PRESERVING

NATURE'S BOUNTY

PRESERVING
NATURE'S BOUNTY

FRANCES BISSELL

Sterling Publishing Co., Inc.
New York

*For my mother, whose crab apple jelly
provided the inspiration.*

AN IMPORTANT NOTE ON MEASUREMENTS

The American pint is used throughout. 16 fluid ounces is equal to 450 millilitres.

Created by Lynn Bryan, The BookMaker, London
Design by Mary Staples
Photography by Amanda Hancocks

Library of Congress Cataloging-in-Publication Data Available

10 9 8 7 6 5 4 3 2 1

Published by Sterling Publishing Co., Inc.
387 Park Avenue South
New York, NY 10016
© 2006 by Frances Bissell

Distributed in Canada by
Sterling Publishing
C/o Canadian Manda Group
165 Dufferin Street
Toronto, Ontario, Canada M6K 3H6

Distributed in the United Kingdom by
GMC Distribution Services
Castle Place, 166 High Street, Lewes
East Sussex, England BN7 1XU

Distributed in Australia by
Capricorn Link (Australia) Pty. Ltd.
P.O. Box 704, Windsor
NSW 2756, Australia

Printed in China

Sterling ISBN-13: 978-1-4027-2731-3
ISBN-10: 1-4027-2731-3

For information about custom editions, special sales, premium and
corporate purchases, please contact Sterling Special Sales
Department at 800-805-5489 or specialsales@sterlingpub.com.

CONTENTS

INTRODUCTION

Preserving foodstuffs in times of plenty to provide nourishment during lean times has always been a part of the human experience. Making strawberry jam after a summer visit to a roadside farm stand is a throwback to those times when our ancestors canned the summer glut of fruit and vegetables for use throughout winter. Of course we can buy strawberries from every part of the globe in winter, but who would buy expensive, and often tasteless, out-of-season strawberries to use in jam? No, the pleasure of making jam and other preserves is that we make them in season, when the fruit is at its sweet, ripe peak and prices are at their lowest. That way we can stash away a thrifty hoard of gleaming jars on our shelves, to give to family and friends as presents, or to brighten up the breakfast table with a jar of homemade Lemon Curd (page 71), or the barbecued ribs with a pot of Fennel and Chili Jelly (page 136).

The smell of sugar and fruit cooking in a large saucepan was a delicious part of my childhood, even though I can remember complaining about being scratched when we were sent off to pick wild blackberries in late summer. And I can remember being scornful of the pale, translucent coral jelly my mother made from crab apples. Why could we not have store-bought jam, like my school friends? When I had a kitchen of my own, and someone beloved to cook for, however, I soon realized the joys of making my own preserves, and the pleasure they give friends and family.

I also like to make jams and jellies when staying in friends' houses. It makes me feel at home, and it means I leave behind a present "for the house." In this fashion I have made pear and Chianti jam in Tuscany; crab apple jelly and blueberry jam in Pennsylvania; quince jelly in Connecticut; lemon curd, sun-dried tomatoes, and persimmon jam in Gozo. Often I do not have the proper equipment, especially for jelly making, and I can confirm that the upturned stool with a scalded, clean dish towel or pillowcase suspended from the legs makes an adequate jelly bag and rack.

Sometimes I bring the ingredients home with me, carefully cradling persimmons from Cesena, or cherries from Vignola; lemons from the Amalfi coast, bergamots and Seville

oranges from Andalucia. Before my bags are unpacked, I haul out the jam pan and the hoarded jars. Cleaning copper is not my favorite pastime, so you will not find an array of copper pots and pans in my kitchen, but I do treasure a sturdy copper preserving pan.

However, my book is not about filling shelves and shelves with homemade preserves. Who among us has that kind of space in our kitchen? And who wants to spend hours chopping bushels of apples? No, this is about using what fresh fruits and vegetables you might find in your local farmers' market one Saturday morning, or what friends might bring you from their country home. It's about thinking beyond a fruit salad or a smoothie, and considering how you might preserve those rich, ripe flavors for a while longer. It's about planning ahead to give friends an edible treat for a birthday or Christmas, something that is all your own work. It is easy, I promise you.

There are no recipes calling for 10 pounds of tomatoes, or a bushel of peaches. With just a pound of fruit, you can make two to three small jars of exquisite jelly. I use basic, traditional methods; there are no shortcuts to making fine products. The first chapter will get you started, with information on equipment and basic ingredients, and comments on tried-and-tested techniques for making jams, jellies, chutneys, pickles, marmalades, salsa, and ketchups, as well as fruit-flavored vodkas and syrups.

The book is organized in three sections: Fruits, such as apples, persimmons, and oranges; Vegetables, such as beets, bell peppers, and tomatoes (here, even though they are, strictly speaking, a fruit); and Making Christmas Preserves, including Cranberry and Cinnamon Jelly and a very good mincemeat. These are delightful to make because they can be given as gifts to loved ones. All you need to become expert at preserving is an afternoon free from distractions, the fruits and vegetables of your choice, and patience to read the recipe carefully. Remember, the more you try it, the better you will become at preserving Nature's seasonal gluts.

FRANCES BISSELL

CANNING TECHNIQUES & EQUIPMENT

Sugar, salt, vinegar, and alcohol are all natural preservatives. We can use them alone, or in combination, and they all work in the same way, by providing a hostile environment for the bacteria, yeasts, and mold that otherwise cause spoilage and fermentation in jams, jellies, pickles, chutneys, and all the other delicious homemade preserves.

Water is the perfect medium to encourage bacteria to grow, and as fruit and vegetables are largely made up of water, the object in preserving them is to replace the water with a high concentration of sugar, vinegar, salt, or alcohol in various combinations, or, in the case of drying, to remove the water altogether. Long, slow cooking also aids this process because water is evaporated during cooking.

Chutneys, which are generally cooked for a long time, release much of their water content and can get by with less vinegar than pickles. The reason for this is that most pickles are raw or only lightly cooked and, therefore, need a heavy dose of vinegar to preserve them, as well as an initial brine bath to draw out the water.

Jams and jellies have about an equal proportion of fruit and sugar; a high sugar concentration helps to ensure mold will not occur, except when using low-sugar pectin (*see page 13*).
Do not be tempted to reduce the sugar content of any of these preserves, with the aim of reducing calories. A reduction in sugar can lead to fermentation, spoilage, and mold.

DIFFERENT TYPES OF PRESERVES, THEIR CHARACTERISTICS & SPECIFIC REQUIREMENTS

JAM

This is a simple preserve of fruit cooked until soft, usually with a little water, then sugar is added and the mixture boiled until the setting point is reached at 220°F. It is important not to cook the fruit and sugar beyond its setting point, or the sugar will caramelize and the fruit flavor will be much diminished.

Jam is ready to use as soon as it has cooled and set. It should be stored in a cool, dry place and used within 12 months.

TO TEST JAM AND JELLY FOR A SET WITHOUT A THERMOMETER

The mixture will begin to look like jam after about 10 minutes, with a slightly thicker texture and slightly darker appearance then when you started cooking the mixture. The fruit will also begin to take on a more translucent appearance as it absorbs the sugar.

To test for the setting point, remove the pan from the heat. The setting point is reached when the jam begins to fall off the wooden spoon in a long "curtain" rather than single drops. You can also drop a little of the hot mixture on a cold saucer. When the jam is cold, push it gently with your finger. If it wrinkles, the jam or jelly has reached its setting point and is ready to be potted. This is sometimes called "sheeting."

SETTING POINT

The temperature for a setting point depends on the altitude of where you live:

ALTITUDE	TEMPERATURE
Sea level	220°F
1,000 feet	218°F
2,000 feet	216°F
3,000 feet	214°F
4,000 feet	212°F
5,000 feet	211°F
6,000 feet	209°F
7,000 feet	207°F
8,000 feet	205°F

JELLY

As a general rule, pectin-rich fruit will take about 2 cups or 1 pound of sugar to 2 cups extracted juice; fruit lower in pectin will need only about 1½ cups sugar per 2 cups juice. With pectin-rich fruit, such as quince, you can take a second extract. Let the first boiling drip through a scalded jelly bag for about 20 minutes only. Return the fruit pulp to the pan, with half the water initially used, and simmer for 30 minutes longer, and then leave to drip for an hour or so.

Note that yields for jellies are approximate, as this depends on the ripeness of the fruit, and whether one or two extracts are taken.

Jellies are ready to use as soon as they have cooled and set. Store them in a cool, dry place and use within 12 months.

FRUIT BUTTER AND FRUIT CHEESE

These are traditional, rural preserves, made when there is a glut of apples, plums, or other fruit. A large quantity of fruit is needed for a relatively small yield, as the fruit pulp is cooked with sugar until it has the consistency of heavy cream, for fruit butter, and to a very stiff paste for fruit cheese. The latter is potted in small, sterilized jars and kept for at least three to four months for the flavors to develop, and fruit butter is potted like jam and is ready to use when it is cool.

FRUIT CURD

Sharp fruit juice, such as citrus or passion fruit, is blended to a velvety texture and rich taste with eggs and butter in this most luxurious preserve. Because fresh eggs and butter are used, this is a preserve that must be refrigerated, not stored in a cupboard, and should be used within four weeks. It can, however, be frozen successfully for three to four months.

Use the freshest possible eggs because even though they undergo some heat treatment, it is not enough to kill bacteria, and they should be regarded as being raw. Therefore the usual warnings about consumption of raw and partially cooked eggs apply. People with low immunity deficiency, the very old, the very young, and pregnant women should not eat fruit curds.

FRUIT SYRUP AND CORDIAL

These "liquid fruits" make refreshing drinks in summer, diluted with still or sparkling mineral water, and can be used to make creative cocktails. They are also delicious poured over ice cream. Apricots, blackberries, cherries, dates, grapes, and mulberries are some of the fruit you can use, as well, of course, as lemons and limes, to make a syrup and a cordial.

Because pectin is not required in the making of syrup, you can use ripe, almost overripe, fruit provided it is not spoiled in any way. The technique is simple. The cleaned fruit is cooked in just enough water to let the juices to run free, then the fruit is mashed, and the pulp squeezed, not dripped, through a scalded jelly bag or cheesecloth. Use 2 cups sugar added per 2 cups liquid.

Do not keep syrups for longer than 12 months as color and flavor begin to deteriorate after that, even when stored in a cool, dark place.

To prevent syrups and cordials from fermenting, they must be sterilized in the bottle, using the boiling-water bath method. The same method is used for ketchups, as described below.

Boiling-water bath to sterilize syrups and bottled ketchup

Sterilize corks, caps, and stoppers by boiling them in water to cover by 2 inches for 15 minutes. Use a funnel to fill the bottle to 1½ inches below the bottom of the cork or screwcap. Corks need to be tied or security wired in place or the heat will force them out. Put the bottles in a deep saucepan, and add enough water to come to the bottom of the cork. Bring the water to a boil, cover the pan, and maintain the water at a steady boil for 20 minutes. Turn off the heat, and using tongs, remove the bottles from the water and stand them on a wooden tray to cool. Label and store them in a cool, dark place.

FRUIT RATAFIA, LIQUEUR, AND FLAVORED VODKA

Unlike syrups and cordials, these preserves contain alcohol. Each is made by macerating the fruit and its peel in the spirit, to draw out the flavor compounds. The liquor is then bottled to produce an unsweetened but fragrant spirit. To make a fruit liqueur, crush the fruit, strain off the juices, mix with sugar, and then add spirit. All of these are useful in cocktails, as well as to splash on ice creams or sorbets. They can also be used to enhance fruit tarts and mousses.

MARMALADE

Marmalade making is not difficult, just time consuming, thus it is worth making plenty of it. All you need is a large saucepan, a large measuring jug, a large weighing bowl on your kitchen scales, a long-handled spoon, suitable jars and closures, and patience. Using the basic recipe on page 43, you will be left with the glowing satisfaction of having filled jars for your pantry, as well as for presents. Store them in a cool, dry place and use within 12 months. Marmalade is ready to eat as soon as it is cold and set. Like all fruit preserves, marmalade will darken as it matures.

Quantities in marmalade recipes can never be exact. You might, for example, simmer the oranges longer than I simmer them; they might need it if they are less than fresh, and more water will evaporate in the cooking; you might push more pulp through your strainer than I do, which affects the overall yield. Your oranges might contain more juice and/or pectin than mine. If you use too small a pan, you will have to stop the mixture boiling occasionally to prevent it bubbling over. All this affects cooking time and quantities of sugar and water.

CHUTNEY

Chutneys are among my favorite preserves, with deep, rich fruit and vegetable flavors and strong, hot notes of chili and vinegar. Preserved with vinegar, salt, and sugar, chutneys simply require long, slow cooking. The mixture does not "gel" but thickens as the water evaporates. A heat-diffusing mat is useful to maintain a low simmer without burning the contents of the pan. When making preserves that require vinegar to be cooked, it is best to open the kitchen windows. The smell of cooking vinegar is very pervasive.

All chutneys are best kept for at least two months before using. Traditionally they were made in the fall and opened at Christmas, being the perfect accompaniment to holiday buffets and platters of cold cuts. However, they are good enough to be eaten a few days after they have been made. They are also excellent to eat with broiled and barbecued meats.

PICKLE

One of the differences between a chutney and a pickle is that generally chutney is made with sugar, and pickles are generally made without. However, I like to use sugar in some of my pickles, so I do not know if this makes them chuckles or pickneys. Also, pickles are made from raw or lightly cooked vegetables, and are therefore crisp.

▨ Ideally, pickles should be kept for a month before using, and consumed within 12 months.

KETCHUP

A finely balanced combination of fruit, or vegetable, with sugar, vinegar, and spices, ketchups are an excellent addition to the array of homemade preserves. Kiwifruit or mango ketchup can be used in just the same way as you might use tomato ketchup, but both are infinitely more exotic. You can make them for immediate use, and for storing in the refrigerator for a few weeks, but to keep ketchup for a few months, it must be processed in a boiling-water bath (page 20). The reason is that unlike chutneys and pickles, the concentration of sugar and vinegar is too low to act as a preservative. And you cannot increase the quantities without overpowering the flavor of the fruit or vegetable.

SALSA

Most salsa recipes are a mixture of low-acid vegetables and fruit, such as onions, chilies, bell peppers, mangoes, and pineapples, combined with more acidic ingredients such as tomatoes. Sugar might or might not be used and herbs and spices are often added for extra flavor. Salsas will keep in the refrigerator for a few weeks, but if you are using up a glut of tomatoes or other ingredients, you will be making larger quantities and will want to store the jars for longer, so process them in a boiling-water bath.

Use only high-quality tomatoes, mangoes, and other fruit, at their peak, neither underripe nor overripe. The ingredients used in salsa help preserve it. Acid must be added when making a salsa for storing, because the natural acidity in the tomatoes might not be high enough. Spices and herbs add flavor to salsas, and cilantro and cumin are those most often used, although I like to use fresh mint occasionally.

INGREDIENTS REQUIRED IN MAKING PRESERVES

ALCOHOL

For preserving fruit, such as the Rumtopf recipe on page 169, and making flavored liqueurs and spirits, such as the Cranberry Vodka on page 46, a neutral inexpensive vodka is best; you do not need to invest in a premium brand.

PECTIN

This is a form of carbohydrate contained in the cell walls of fruit and is the substance that makes jam and jelly set, or "gel," when combined with sugar. As the fruit ripens, the pectin diminishes, so it is important to choose fruit that is just ripe or slightly underripe. Overripe fruit is often sold at bargain prices, but it will not set well, and is therefore not an economy.

Some fruits contain plenty of pectin; others have far less and require the addition of extra pectin, in the form of pectin-rich fruit, or liquid or powdered pectin. Liquid or powdered pectin is made from apple or citrus trimmings, such as peel, seeds, and pith; the best is made from apple. It is sold in packages of about 1½ oz, and directions for use, including cooking times, are given on the packet. These directions should be followed. You can also purchase low-sugar pectins that require less sugar than the standard jam or jelly recipe. It is most important to follow the manufacturer's directions.

Acidity is also required to assist the combination of pectin and sugar into a gel and this generally correlates with pectin; where this is high, the acidity is also high, except for pomegranates, which are low in pectin but have medium to high acidity. Citrus fruits are high in acidity, as are black, red, and white currants, and, surprisingly, plums. Lemon juice is used to provide any extra acidity needed; you can also use bottled lemon juice in place of freshly squeezed juice in any of the recipes, except, of course, the recipes requiring fresh lemons.

A GUIDE TO THE PECTIN CONTENT OF FRUIT

High: Apples, clementines, crab apples, cranberries, currants (black, red, and white), damsons, gooseberries, grapefruit, guavas, kumquats, lemons, limes, oranges, plums, and quinces

Medium: Apricots, blackberries, blueberries, grapes, greengage plums, loganberries, prickly pears, raspberries, and tomatoes

Low: Cherries, figs, kiwifruit, litchis, mangoes, melons, passion fruit, peaches, pears, pineapples, pomegranates, rhubarb, and strawberries

---

SUGAR

Granulated sugar, an excellent all-round sugar, can be used whatever preserves you are making. For chutneys, which are generally thick, opaque, and dark, you can use an unrefined sugar, such as Demerara, soft light brown sugar, or light muscovado sugar. These unrefined sugars can usually be found in health-food stores and specialist food stores.

SALT

My favorite salt is coarse sea salt, and I use this in my chutneys, pickles, and salsa, both for the brine bath for pickles, and the flavoring. Kosher salt and preserving salt can also be used. The reason for choosing a coarse salt, especially when brining, is that it does not contain the anticaking additives found in many brands of fine salt, which can lead to distorted flavors and cloudiness in the brine.

ACID

Commonly used acids are vinegar and lemon juice. Lemon juice is more acidic than vinegar, but has less effect on flavor, and you can use bottled lemon juice.

The vinegar used should be at least five percent acid. Pickles are best made with distilled vinegar, as it is strong and clear in color. Chutneys can use one of the darker vinegars, such as cider vinegar or red wine vinegar. There is, however, a huge range of vinegars to choose from now, and it is worth experimenting. Sherry vinegar, for example, is dark and strong, and will add distinction to your chutneys; muscatel vinegar, made from sweet wine, is a delicate product, and useful when making spiced fruit preserves and more delicate chutneys. Non-brewed condiment is to be avoided. This might be white or brown. The former is simply water and acetic acid; the latter has added caramel for coloring.

Acid is corrosive when in direct contact with metal, therefore when you pot pickles and chutneys, you should make sure that you are using vinegarproof lids. This is one case where it is probably worth investing in new preserving jars, especially as some of the recipes need to be boiling-water processed for longer storing.

AN IMPORTANT NOTE ON ALMONDS, APRICOTS, PEACHES, AND SOME OTHER TREE FRUIT

Do not include the kernels when making apricot, peach, or plum jam, nor use bitter almonds. Instead use pure almond extract. The cyanogenic glycosides present in bitter almonds, and in the kernels of apricots, peaches, plums, and nectarines, as well as apple and pear seeds, are unlikely to be destroyed by cooking. The kernels contain significant amounts of these compounds, and as they are natural products, the amount they contain varies. Despite what many cookbooks state, these toxins are not destroyed in cooking, and as a general practice we should not be adding cyanide to our food.

Ordinary "sweet" almonds, however, are safe to use; except, of course, for those persons having nut allergies.

Here are a couple of useful vinegar recipes for pickling. You can adapt the spicing if you want to create new recipes.

SWEET VINEGAR

MAKES 1 QUART

1	quart white wine vinegar
1	cinnamon stick
4	cloves
4	crushed cardamom pods
5 cups	sugar

Put the vinegar and spices in a nonreactive saucepan and bring to a boil. Stir in the sugar and, when it dissolves, boil for 1 minute. Remove from the heat, cover, and leave to infuse for 3 to 4 hours. Use as directed, or bottle and seal it for future use. It will keep for at least 12 months without further processing.

SPICED VINEGAR

MAKES 1 QUART

1 quart	distilled vinegar
1 teaspoon	black peppercorns
1 teaspoon	allspice berries
1 teaspoon	coriander seeds
1 teaspoon	cumin seeds
1 teaspoon	blade mace
1	cinnamon stick
4	cloves
4	crushed green cardamom pods
1 teaspoon	salt
1 cup	sugar

Put the vinegar, spices, and salt in a a nonreactive saucepan and bring to a boil. Stir in the sugar and, when it dissolves, boil for 1 minute. Remove from the heat, cover, and leave to infuse for 3 to 4 hours. Use as directed, or bottle and seal it for future use. It will keep for 12 months without further processing.

EQUIPMENT REQUIRED FOR MAKING PRESERVES

CANDY THERMOMETER

A thermometer is the surest way of testing when jam and jelly has reached its setting point. The temperature, at sea level, will be 220°F / 105°C. *See Jam.*

CHEESECLOTH FOR TYING HERBS & SPICES

When flavoring preserves with herbs and spices that you want to remove before potting, it is a good idea to tie them in a small square of scalded cheesecloth, so they can easily be removed. Buy a yard of cheesecloth and cut it into small squares to keep on hand for this purpose.

JARS & BOTTLES

▒ There is a great temptation to save jam and mayonnaise jars and pretty bottles for future use, but the scope for doing this is very limited.

▒ Keep in mind that room-temperature storage of sealed jars of all preserves means all jars should undergo processing in a boiling water bath in order to destroy bacteria, prevent mold and spoilage, and prolong their shelf life. Thus you need specially tempered strong glass jars. The standard canning jar, of the Mason type, has a threaded neck, a self-sealing flat metal lid with nonmetallic lining and integral gasket, and a screw band. It comes in half-pint and pint sizes.

▒ It is easy to tell that the boiling-water bath processing, details of which are on page 20, has been successful and a vacuum has been formed, because the lid will depress in the middle. When the lid is prized off to open the jar, the vacuum is broken and the lid "pops."

▒ The jars can be reused, as can the screw bands, but new lids must be used for every new batch of preserves.

▒ The United States Department of Agriculture (USDA) has advised that jars with a glass lid, rubber sealing ring, and metal ring and clamp are no longer considered suitable, despite their still being available and in use, both commercially and domestically.

▒ If you are making preserves for presents, fairs, or fund-raisers it is strongly advised that you use the USDA recommended jars.

A sugar thermometer, plastic strainers, cheesecloth squares, kitchen tongs, and a large glass mixing bowl are among the essentials items you need for preserving fruits and vegetables.

■ Vinegars, flavored vodkas, and liqueurs are not heat processed, and for these you can use pre-used bottles provided they have been thoroughly washed, in soapy water, rinsed, and sterilized first, following one of the methods described below.

■ Syrups and cordials to be stored at room temperature should be bottled in new glass bottles suitable for boiling-water bath processing.

■ Some pickles, such as cucumbers and onions, are not processed in a boiling-water bath, because it is essential to keep them crisp. These should be stored in the refrigerator, where they will keep for 6 to 9 months, and for these you can use pre-used jars, provided they have first been thoroughly washed in soapy water, rinsed, and sterilized, following one of the methods below.

■ All jars, lids, corks, and closures should be sterilized before use.

■ For domestic use, it is still possible, in many places, to buy the simplest seals for jam and jelly jars, which are wax disks and cellophane covers secured with a rubber band. However, the USDA has advised paraffin wax does not provide an adequate seal. *See www.usda.gov*

TO STERILIZE JAM JARS

If you are preparing a large batch of preserves, the easiest way is to put everything in the dishwasher and run it on the hottest cycle. When the cycle is over, use tongs to transfer the hot jars to the countertop covered with a clean dish towel.

Alternatively, place jars and lids in boiling water to cover by 2 inches for 15 minutes. Or, you can use the oven. Heat it to 220°F, put the jars and lids in, and leave them for 15 minutes. Switch the oven off and leave the jars inside until you are ready to fill them with hot preserves. If filling the jars with cold preserves, such as pickles, remove them from the oven as soon as they have been sterilized to allow them to cool before filling. Again, use tongs to remove them and place on a covered countertop ready to receive the preserves.

JAM FUNNEL

This wide-mouthed funnel is a useful gadget in that it sits inside the neck of the jar you are filling, thus avoiding sticky spills down the side and on the neck, as well as splashed hands. If you bottle syrups, ketchups, and cordials, it is also useful to have a small funnel that fits inside a bottle neck.

JELLY BAG & RACK

This is a cheesecloth bag designed to be suspended from a four-cornered plastic rack that you secure on the rim of a large wide bowl or pitcher. The bag is first scalded with boiling water before being suspended, and then you ladle in the cooked fruit pulp when making jelly. The cheesecloth is fine enough to let just the clear liquid drip through, ensuring a bright jelly.

It is possible to improvise and tie a thin, scalded dish towel from the four legs of an upturned stool, with the bowl in the middle. I have done this countless times, and it works perfectly well.

LARGE SAUCEPAN WITH LID & TRIVET

This is essential equipment for the boiling-water bath in which preserves are processed to give them longer shelf life. You can also use a fish kettle, as this has a false bottom that keeps the jars from the bottom of the pan, so they are not in contact with direct heat. Small ½-pint or squat 1-pint jars will fit a fish kettle, which is useful because it fits across two burners on the stovetop and will hold several jars. Buy boiling-water canners specifically for home-canning.

LONG-HANDLED WOODEN SPOON

This lets you stir the mixture with less risk of the hot mixture splashing your hand or arm.

NONREACTIVE BOWL

It is best to use a glass or plastic bowl for brine baths or for soaking ingredients in vinegar overnight when making pickles, as these do not corrode when in contact with salt and acid.

NONREACTIVE SAUCEPAN

Because of the amount of acid in fruit, and with the addition of vinegar for chutneys and pickles, it is essential to use a pan which will not corrode. The best are heavy-gauge stainless steel, which most of us use anyway. They are easy to clean and are good conductors of heat. A copper preserving pan, while attractive, is not essential. Aluminum pans should not be used, because the metal reacts to acidic produce. The best preserving pans are large and wide. The mixture should not come more than halfway up the side of the pan, otherwise it is likely to boil over. A wide surface area aids faster evaporation, therefore the setting point is reached more quickly. You can also use heatproof glass saucepans, but these are not as good heat conductors.

PLASTIC STRAINER

You will need this if you are making ketchup. Once the ingredients have been cooked to a pulp, they need to be rubbed through the strainer before bottling. Because the ketchup contains acid, a metal strainer should not be used.

SLOTTED SPOON

This is for skimming the foam from jam and marmalade mixtures in the saucepan.

TISSUE TEA BAGS FOR HERBS & SPICES

If it is more convenient, use these in place of cheesecloth squares for holding herbs and spices when flavoring preserves. You will find these in specialist stores selling tea and coffee.

TONGS & JAR LIFTER

Use these for handling hot, sterilized jars, and for removing jars from boiling-water baths as required when you process jars using the boiling-water bath method as below.

BOILING-WATER BATH PROCESSING

Most of the preserves will keep in the refrigerator for 2 or 3 months, but if you want to keep them for 12 months or more, then they should be processed in a boiling-water bath, which sterilizes the contents of the jar, and seals them in a vacuum. This method, explained fully below, should also be used for bottling fruit in syrup.

■ Low-acid foods require special processing techniques and equipment for canning or bottling which fall outside the scope of this book.

METHOD

■ Sterilize the glass preserving jars and lids you want to use after first checking there are no chips or cracks on the neck of the jar, because this would prevent a seal from forming. Fill the hot, clean jars with the hot preserve, leaving ¼-inch headspace for jams, jellies, chutneys, and salsas, and ½ inch headspace for fruit and vegetables. Wipe the jar rims with a clean, damp paper towel; anything sticky adhering to the rim prevents the jars from sealing. Put on the lids and screw on the metal bands.

■ Using tongs or a jar lifter, carefully place the jars on a rack or trivet in your selected boiling-water bath (see note on Large Saucepan on page 19), ensuring that the jars do not touch each other or touch the side of the pan. Add more boiling water if necessary to come to 1 to 2 inches above jar tops and bring water to a rolling boil. Set the timer for the recommended processing time. Add boiling water if necessary during the processing to keep the jars covered.

■ The processing time, at sea level, for ½-pint and 1-pint jars of jam and jelly, in presterilized jars, is 5 minutes from the time the water has come back to a boil in the water bath. The processing time at sea level, from boiling, will be 15 minutes for 1-pint jars or bottles of salsa or ketchup, 25 minutes for 1-pint jars of solid ingredients such as peaches. Half-pint jars will need 10 and 15 minutes respectively. 1-quart jars will need 25 and 30 minutes respectively. Add one additional minute for every 1,000 feet above sea level.

■ If processing cold food, covered with cold liquid, also called the cold-pack method, the closed jars are put into cold water, which is brought to a boil, and the processing time is counted from that point.

■ At end of processing time, switch off the heat and, using tongs or a jar lifter, remove the jars from the water bath. Place the jars upright on a rack or work top covered with a clean towel and leave them to cool. Do not tighten the screw bands. As the contents of the jar cool, they shrink and a vacuum is formed, creating a sterile anaerobic or oxygen-free condition in which bacteria will not develop. You can tell the jar is properly sealed if the lid is depressed in the middle and does not move.

■ Remove the screw bands from the sealed jars and wipe the jars with warm, soapy water, then rinse and dry them without disturbing the lid. Make sure the screw bands are clean and dry before you put them away, and they can be reused many times. It is not advisable to leave the bands on the jars, as they can corrode.

■ Label and date the jars then store in a cool, dark, dry place, such as a basement, cellar, or pantry.

■ If a vacuum has not formed, refrigerate the contents of the jar and use as a fresh product, refrigerating and using within a week.

WHAT WENT WRONG

JELLIES & JAMS

The jelly is cloudy
There are several possible causes. The juice was not properly strained and contained particles of pulp. If the fruit was too underripe, it may have set too quickly. The jelly was allowed to stand before being poured into the jars or it was poured in too slowly.

There are crystals in the jelly
You may have used too much sugar in the mixture, or cooked it too slowly, too long, or too little. Crystals may also form on top of a jar of jelly that has been opened and allowed to stand; then the crystals are formed by evaporation. Grape jelly may develop tartrate crystals.

The jelly or jam is too soft
There may be too much juice in the mixture or too little sugar. The acid level in the mixture may not be high enough or you might have cooked too big a batch of fruit at one time.

There is mold on the jelly or jam
Air and, with it, bacteria, has entered the container through an imperfect seal. Do not discard the mold and eat the remainder of the jar's contents, but discard the entire jar. Remember to use recommended canning jars and lids, and process in a boiling-water bath.

PICKLES

Pickles are soft
These should be crunchy. They will be soft if the vegetables were not salted for long enough, or if the salt or vinegar solution was too weak.

Pickles are slippery and soft
Air has got into the pickles through a poor seal and caused spoilage. Or the salt or vinegar solution was not strong enough and bacteria have not been destroyed. Discard the pickles right away.

Pickles are dark and/or cloudy
Table salt with iodine and anti-caking agents was used. Or dark vinegar was used. Or too many spices were added. Using soft water or bottled or filtered water can help keep the pickles bright. Hard water can darken pickles. Reactive utensils such as copper or iron were used.

CHUTNEYS, KETCHUPS & SALSAS

There is mold on the surface
Air and, with it, bacteria has entered the container through an imperfect seal. Do not simply discard the mold and consume the rest of the jar's contents, but discard the entire jar. Remember to always use recommended canning jars and lids, and process in a boiling-water bath.

It doesn't smell good
Any preserve that has an unpleasant or off-putting smell should be discarded immediately.

It appears to be fermenting
Small bubbles appearing around the edges or on the surface indicate that the preserve is fermenting. This may produce harmful toxins and the product should be discarded right away. Fermentation can be caused, depending on the type of preserve, by too little sugar, too weak a brine or vinegar solution, inadequate sterilization of equipment, and too warm storage conditions.

The Boiling-Water Method to Can Fruit

The following recipe is a template for the easy method to can a glut of fresh fruit of the season. In this recipe, I have used peaches.

PEACHES IN SYRUP

FILLS 2 1-QUART JARS

If you want to preserve ripe summer peaches to eat as delicious desserts until the following summer, they should be processed in a boiling-water bath, otherwise they will only keep for a couple of months.

3 pounds	firm, but ripe peaches
2 cups	water
1 cup	sugar

Skin the peaches by putting them in a heatproof bowl and pouring boiling water over them. When cool enough to handle, slip the skins off, halve the fruit, and discard the pit.

Meanwhile, make a thin syrup by boiling the water and sugar without stirring until the sugar dissolves.

Sterilize the glass preserving jars and lids. Although the jars can be used again and again, the lid should be renewed each time you make a batch of fruit in syrup or similar preserves which are processed in a boiling-water bath. It is important that there are no chips or cracks on the neck of the jar, as this prevents a seal from forming.

Pack the fruit into two hot, sterilized 1-quart preserving jars with the inside of the jars still wet. This helps to move the fruit around in the jar to pack it as firmly as possible without squashing it.

Pour the hot syrup over the fruit, and make sure there are not any air bubbles. Gently shake the jar to shift the fruit, or insert a sterilized skewer or knife blade down the side of the jar wherever there are air bubbles. Add more syrup if necessary, so it covers the fruit and reaches to within ½ inch of the neck of the jar, but not far enough for it to touch the lid.

Wipe the rim of the jar, place the lids on, and seal the jars. If using the screw band, give it a quarter turn to loosen it so steam can escape during the sterilization process. Process in a boiling-water bath, page 20. Once the water boils, keep it boiling for 30 minutes (1-pound jars of produce only need 25 minutes), topping up with boiling water if necessary.

Once the jars have been processed, remove the pan from the heat and, with tongs or a jar lifter, remove the jars from the pan and transfer them to a rack or wooden board. Immediately tighten the lids if using screw tops and leave the jars to cool completely. As the contents become cold, they shrink slightly and a vacuum is formed, creating sterile conditions in which bacteria do not survive.

ABOVE The apples are not peeled and cored because pectin is contained in the skin and the seeds.

RIGHT For a clear jelly, leave the pulp to drip through the cheesecloth jelly bag into a clean bowl.

Making Apple Jelly

On these two pages you will see the basic step-by-step process involved in making apple jelly. The process is the same for any fruit that is suitable for a jelly.

APPLE & ROSEMARY JELLY

FILLS 5 1-PINT JARS

Herb and apple jellies are delicious accompaniments to meat, poultry, and game dishes, and can also be used as a glaze, brushed over duck breasts or a pork loin before broiling or roasting. Other herbs can be used in the same way; sage jelly is particularly good, as is lavender jelly.

4 pounds	tart green apples, such as Granny Smith
10 sprigs	rosemary
	juice of 2 lemons
	sugar —*see recipe*

BELOW The clear apple jelly, ready to be stored in the refrigerator for up to 3 months. If you want to store it longer, use the boiling-water bath process.

ABOVE Here, I use a ladle and a nonreactive funnel to make sure the hot jelly is poured into the sterilized jar without mishap.

Wash the apples, cut them into chunks, without peeling or coring, and put in a large, nonreactive saucepan, together with 6 of the rosemary sprigs. Cover with water and simmer until the apples are tender and pulpy, mashing to extract as much juice and flavor as possible. Strain the pulp through a scalded jelly bag suspended over a bowl without squeezing or forcing for several hours, or overnight; otherwise, the jelly will be cloudy. Discard the rosemary sprigs.

Measure the juice and put it into a saucepan. Add 2 cups sugar for each 2 cups liquid. Strain the lemon juice into the saucepan, stirring to dissolve the sugar. Tie 4 sprigs rosemary in a piece of cheesecloth and add the bundle to the saucepan. Bring to a boil, and boil hard for 10 minutes or until the setting point is reached.

Remove the pan from the heat. Using tongs, remove the cheesecloth bundle. Skim and discard any foam from the surface. Pour the jelly into hot, sterilized jars. Seal the jars. Process in a boiling-water bath following the method on page 20. Label the jars and store in a cool, dark place.

FRUIT

Buying fruit

The seasons used to govern our eating and preserving of fruit. We would choose rhubarb in spring, cherries in early summer, soft berry fruits in midsummer, and tree fruits and blackberries in fall, with perhaps a late harvest of raspberries, and then nothing new throughout the winter and spring except stored apples and pears.

As transportation has improved, however, more fruit is available, not just tropical fruit but familiar fruit in the opposite season: strawberries and peaches in December from the southern hemisphere's summer, for example. We might consider ourselves lucky now to have a fruit harvest from all over the world at our disposal, but locally grown fruit, picked when it is ripe and used as soon as possible after picking, is the greatest treat of all.

And it is usually from locally grown sources that we find supplies for turning into preserves, whether from city farmers' markets, roadside farm stands in the country, pick-your-own farms, or your own garden. When you buy or pick fruit for preserves, the specimens should look fresh and appetizing. If the fruit is plump, firm, heavy for its size, and unwrinkled, these are signs of freshness and good moisture or juice content. There are one or two exceptions, however, such as persimmons, which are at their best when bletted, or overripe.

Soft fruit such as berries should look dry and full; avoid those with signs of mold or wetness, including any leakage in the packaging if buying packaged fruit from the supermarket. Whether the fruit skins are edible or inedible, make sure they are not bruised, split, or broken, or show signs of insect damage.

Smell is a good indication of ripeness, which is fortunate because some fruit does need to be bought and used when ripe. All the soft berry fruits fall into this category. Supermarkets now sell fruit in varying stages of ripeness, which they are able to do by using different storage and processing methods, including ethylene gas application, and edible wax coating.

All fruit should be carefully rinsed before making into preserves, to remove any surface traces of pesticides, wax coatings, and others sprays. Warm water and, in the case of harder fruit such as lemons and apples, a clean cloth are sufficient; you do not need to use soap.

If you choose organic fruit and nuts, they will not have chemical pesticide residues, nor will they have been subjected to artificial ripening and preserving processes. The bag of apples might not all be the same shape and size, as they are in the supermarket, but you can eat them in the knowledge you are not adding extra chemicals to your diet. They should, however, still be carefully rinsed; manure is still manure.

Storing fruit

Many fruits ripen successfully at home. Bananas, for example, are often sold pale yellow, tinged with green. These need to be ripened, with the starch changing to sugar, to a warm yellow marked with brown, and will do so if kept in the fruit bowl. Ripe bananas will also ripen any other fruit that is in the fruit bowl with them, because bananas produce ethylene, the ripening agent. Do not refrigerate bananas because their skin will turn black.

Citrus fruit keeps well, for a couple of weeks, if necessary, but the skins will begin to toughen and wrinkle and you will lose some of the essential oils, and moisture. Therefore, if you are making marmalade or curd, use the fruit within a few days. And if you are lucky enough to obtain freshly picked citrus, get the preserving pans out at once. Marmalade made from lemons picked the same day is an incomparable taste experience.

Storing pineapples or melons for preserves is a problem. Their scent is so penetrating they must be well wrapped, or they pass their flavors to other refrigerated foods. Melons should smell of melon, with a characteristic musky fragrance. Although they will keep for a week or so, they will not ripen if bought underripe. Hard fruit, such as apples and pears, as long as they are bought unblemished, will keep for a few weeks in the refrigerator.

Any fruit stored at room temperature will ripen and deteriorate quicker than if stored in a cool place, because the water content gradually evaporates and with it the sweet juiciness that makes the fruit so delicious.

Some fruits, such as raspberries, strawberries, and other soft berry fruits, are best bought for immediate use.

Dried fruit

In itself in a state of preservation, dried fruit can also be used for preserves. Many types of fruit are available dried. While fruit in its natural state is bursting with fresh, sweet juice, once dried it changes character completely. It becomes dense, concentrated in flavor, and often not very attractive to look at, being wrinkled and leathery. Dried fruit is sometimes treated with sulfur dioxide to help preserve it further. Fruit that has been treated as such will be identifiable from the label. In an airtight container in a cool, dry, well-ventilated place, dried fruit will keep for up to 18 months.

PRESERVES MADE WITH DRIED FRUIT

Vine fruits

Currants, golden raisins, and raisins are all dried grapes: currants are black grapes, sultanas are green, and raisins vary depending on the grape type. While they can be soaked and cooked, vine fruits are most often used in their dried, concentrated form. They are particularly useful in the traditional Christmas preserve, mincemeat.

Tree fruits

Reconstituted, fruits such as apricots, prunes, apples, peaches, and nectarines can be used as you would the fresh, in jams and jellies, and also in chutneys, pickles, and salsas.

Other dried fruits

Although dried dates and figs are often eaten as they are, both are excellent chopped up, mixed with nuts and spices, and added to a mincemeat mixture. They can also be useful as a standby to make jam.

Apples

If you pick your own apples and need to store them, treat them carefully. The apples should be perfect and free of blemishes; handle them as little as possible in picking and packing. Place them in trays, not touching, or in baskets, or indeed in plastic bags with a couple of ventilation holes, then store in a cool, dry place.

■ Because of their high pectin content, apples are useful in making preserves in that they can be combined with other fruit low in pectin, such as cherries, mangoes, and greengage plums. In addition, apples can provide a basic jelly that you can then flavor with herbs, spices, or flowers.

■ Apples grow in temperate climates in the northern and southern hemispheres, so we have apples all year round. Homegrown apples ripen from midsummer onward. Unlike later-ripening apples and cooking apples, which have good keeping qualities, these early apples do not store well, and should be used right away.

■ Despite the hundreds of apple varieties still being grown, you often have to make do with only a handful of varieties in the stores. Nevertheless, these are perfectly good for using in preserves, pickles and chutneys—Granny Smith, Golden Delicious, Greening, Jonagold, Northern Spy, Spartan, Braeburn, Fuji, McIntosh, Empire, Pink Lady, Paula Red, Ida Red, and Gala are the most commonly available apples. These may not all be available in supermarkets, but are apples to look for in farmers' markets or pick-your-own farms.

APPLE, EARL GREY TEA & ALMOND JELLY

FILLS 4 1-PINT JARS

This is a pale, elegant jelly, with a subtle flavor, which shows at its best with warm scones or biscuits for a traditional British afternoon tea.

3 pounds	tart green apples such as Granny Smith
2 tablespoons	loose Earl Grey tea
	sugar—*see recipe*
3/4 cup	slivered almonds
1/2 teaspoon	pure almond extract

Wash the apples, cut them into chunks without peeling or coring, and put in a large nonreactive saucepan, together with half the tea wrapped in a cheesecloth bag. Cover with water and simmer until the apples are tender and pulpy, mashing to extract as much juice and flavor as possible. Suspend a scalded jelly bag or large scalded piece of cheesecloth over a bowl. Strain the pulp through the bag without squeezing and let it drip for several hours or overnight.

Measure the juice and put it in a saucepan. Measure an equal volume of sugar, allowing 2 cups sugar to each 2 cups juice. Add the rest of the tea, in another cheesecloth bag. Simmer gently until the sugar dissolves. Bring the liquid to a rapid boil and boil until the setting point is reached.

Remove the pan from the heat and discard the bag of tea. Skim any foam from the surface of the jelly and allow to stand for a few minutes before stirring in the almonds and almond extract. Ladle the hot jelly into sterilized hot jars. Seal. Process in a boiling-water bath, following the method on page 20. Label the jars. Store in a cool, dark place. Use within 12 months.

SPICED APPLE & PEAR BUTTER

FILLS 5 ½-PINT JARS

Although traditionally made with apples, I like to use a combination of apples and pears, for a richer, more complex flavor. Try serving it warm, perhaps with a dash of calvados or poire William, *over vanilla ice cream.*

8	tart apples, such as Granny Smith, peeled, cored, and chopped
8	pears, such as Bartlett, Seckel or Williams, peeled, cored, and chopped
1 cup	apple juice
1 cup	pear juice
2	large cinnamon sticks
4	thin slices fresh gingerroot
12	allspice berries
8	cloves
	seeds of 4 cardamom pods
3 cups	sugar

Put the apples and pears and both juices in a nonreactive saucepan, with the spices, including ginger, tied in scalded cheesecloth. Simmer for about an hour until the fruit is tender. Remove the bundle of spices and, with a stick blender, blend the fruit until smooth, or rub it through a sieve into another nonreactive saucepan. Stir in the sugar and put back the bundle of spices. When the sugar has dissolved, simmer the mixture until it thickens, about 40 minutes. Remove the pan from the heat and, with tongs, discard the spice bundle and fill hot, sterilized jars with the butter. Seal and process according to the instructions on page 20. Label the jars. Store in a cool, dry place and use within 12 months.

COOK'S NOTE: *You can apply this method when making any fruit butters, depending on availability. Consider a luscious peach or apricot butter in summer, or a plum and pear butter later in the season.*

Apricot

This small blushing fruit has given its name to one of the sunniest, most delicate colors of the spectrum, a subtle mix of pink, yellow, and orange. Pale, or tinged with green, the fruit will be firmer and underripe. The skin of the apricot is soft and tender with a mat bloom. The flesh is juicy, slightly firmer than that of a peach, and usually the same color as the skin. The large, brown, inedible pit should be discarded. The apricot kernel housed in the pit should not be added to the apricot preserve. See page 14 for an explanation.

PITTING FRUIT

To remove the pit from fruits such as apricots, nectarines, and peaches, cut around the middle of the fruit through the crease with a sharp knife. Firmly twist the halves against each other and lever out the pit.

APRICOT JAM WITH MUSCATEL WINE

FILLS 5 1-PINT JARS

3 pounds	ripe apricots
4 tablespoons	lemon juice
2 cups	muscatel wine—such as *Beaumes de Venise, Moscato d'Asti,* or orange Muscat
7 1/2 cups	sugar

Rinse and dry the apricots, cut each in half, and remove the pit, then quarter the flesh. Put the flesh in a saucepan with the wine and lemon juice and simmer until the fruit is soft. Stir in the sugar, and after it dissolves, boil briskly until the setting point is reached.

Remove the pan from the heat. Skim any foam from the surface. Pot the jam in hot, sterilized jars. Seal. Process in a boiling-water bath, following the method on page 20. Label the jars, and store in a cool, dark place. Use within 12 months.

COOK'S NOTE: *For a variation, replace the wine with water and stir in a few drops of pure almond extract and a couple of handfuls slivered almonds after the pan is removed from the heat. Do not use the apricot kernels.*

Blackberries

A sweet, black, juicy fruit made up of tiny drupelets, the blackberry grows throughout the United States. It grows wild in woodlands and hedgerows from high summer to the first frosts.

■ Wild blackberries have a delicious sweet yet tart flavor, are small and firm, and have rather a lot of seed to flesh. Cultivated blackberries taste almost as good and are rather more fleshy and juicy. When buying, look for firm, glossy black fruit without any green and red patches and without any sign of mold.

BLACKBERRY, CINNAMON & PINOT NOIR JELLY

FILLS 6 ½-PINT JARS

This makes a very sophisticated afternoon snack, spread on hot toast, playing on some of the flavors that can be detected in a glass of pinot noir.

2 pounds	blackberries
1¼ cups	pinot noir wine
1	cinnamon stick
	juice of 1 lemon
	sugar—*see recipe*

Put the fruit, wine, cinnamon, and lemon juice in a saucepan and simmer until the fruit is soft. Crush it with a potato masher, before spooning it into a scalded jelly bag suspended over a bowl or a large pitcher and letting it drip, without squeezing or forcing, for several hours or overnight.

The next day, measure the juice and put it in a nonreactive saucepan. Stir in 2 cups sugar for each 2 cups juice. Heat gently until the sugar dissolves, then boil briskly until the setting point is reached. Remove the pan from the heat. Skim any foam from the surface. Pour the jelly into hot, sterilized jars. Seal. Process in a boiling-water bath, following the method on page 20. Label the jars, and store in a cool, dark place. Use within 12 months.

BLACKBERRY VINEGAR

FILLS 2 1-PINT BOTTLES

Made using the same maceration technique as the blackberry vodka (below), blackberry vinegar makes a good addition to a salad dressing, and can also be used for deglazing the pan when you are cooking pork, poultry, or game.

| 2 pounds | ripe blackberries |
| 1 quart | white wine vinegar |

Put the fruit in a nonreactive bowl and pour the vinegar over. Crush the fruit with a potato masher, and leave, covered, for 48 hours. Strain through cheesecloth into a pitcher, then decant into bottles. Cork and label the bottle.

BLACKBERRY VODKA

FILLS 1 LARGE VODKA BOTTLE

Blackberry vodka is easy to make, and a spoonful of this turns a glass of dry sparkling white wine into an excellent cocktail.

2 pounds	ripe blackberries
	sugar, to taste—*optional*
1 quart	vodka

Mash the blackberries in a bowl, adding sugar if you prefer a sweet cordial. Pour the vodka over, cover with plastic wrap, and leave in a cool place for 48 hours.

Stir, then strain the liquid into a sterilized bottle through a funnel lined with cheesecloth. Cork and label. Store in the refrigerator.

Blueberries

The blueberry has several cousins, including bilberry, blaeberry, whinberry, and whortleberry, all harvested throughout the summer to early Fall. The blueberry flavor is sharp, yet sweet and fragrant. Blueberries make excellent jam and jelly, particularly when mixed with a fruit richer in pectin, or combined with plenty of freshly squeezed lemon juice.

■ Blueberries keep rather better than the other soft fruits, and undamaged specimens will last for a few days in the refrigerator, and they freeze very well, so it is worth buying them in late summer when prices at their lowest, although they are never very cheap. For this reason, I generally turn them into jam, which is more economical than jelly.

BLUEBERRY JAM

FILLS 5 1-PINT JARS

As well as going nicely with the breakfast toast or croissants, blueberry jam is a delicious topping for ice cream, and it can be stirred it into a bowl of plain yogurt.

3 pounds	blueberries, rinsed
2 tablespoons	water
6 cups	sugar
4 tablespoons	lemon juice

Put the fruit in a nonreactive saucepan with the water and simmer until the fruit is soft. Add the sugar and lemon juice and stir gently until the sugar dissolves, then boil briskly until the setting point is reached.

Remove the pan from the heat. Skim any foam from the surface, and leave the jam to cool slightly, 10 to 15 minutes. Stir to distribute the fruit evenly, then pot in hot, sterilized jars. Seal. Process in a boiling-water bath, following the method on page 20. Label the jars, and store in a cool, dark place. Use within 12 months.

Cherries

Sharp, sweet, fleshy fruit with juice that stains your lips, your fingers, and everything it comes in contact with, cherries are a summertime treat worth waiting for. When shopping for cherries examine the stems as these are good indicators of freshness: they should be green and flexible. Dry, brown, brittle stems tell you the cherries were picked some time ago.

■ Red varieties are ripe when they are deep red; white and yellow varieties when they are flushed with pink. Avoid fruit that is too soft, or bruised, or split, and do not keep cherries for more than two to three days, or up to six days in the refrigerator.

CHERRY JAM

FILLS 4 1-PINT JARS

Cherry jam makes a perfect filling, with or without whipped cream, for a chocolate cake. And it is good with breakfast toast. Strawberry jam can be made in the same way.

6 cups	sugar *(a little less if the fruit is very sweet)*
2/3 cup	raspberry juice
2/3 cup	red currant juice, squeezed and strained from the fresh fruit
3 pounds	pitted cherries
	juice of 1 lemon, strained

Put the sugar and half the raspberry and red currant juices in a nonreactive saucepan and simmer, stirring gently until the sugar dissolves. Add the remaining juice and pour everything over the cherries in a heatproof nonreactive bowl or saucepan and leave overnight. The next day, bring everything to a boil, including the lemon juice, and boil rapidly until the setting point is reached. Remove the pan from the heat. Skim any foam from the surface. Leave to stand 10 to 15 minutes and then stir to distribute the fruit. Spoon the jam into sterilized, hot jars. Seal. Process in a boiling-water bath, following the method on page 20. Label the jars, and store in a cool, dark place. Use within 12 months.

COOK'S NOTE: *Cherries and strawberries are low in pectin and need the added pectin to be found in red currant juice.*

Here are two recipes I learned from Meni, my Greek friend. The preserve is a softer-setting mixture than the cherry jam in the previous recipe.

CHERRY PRESERVE (GREEK VISINO)

FILLS 2 1-PINT JARS

This is perfect stirred into thick Greek-style yogurt.

2 pounds	cherries, pitted
2 cups	sugar
	juice of 1/2 lemon

Leave the sugar and cherries to macerate in a covered bowl overnight. (Reduce the amount of sugar by about a fifth if the cherries are very sweet.)

Transfer the fruit and sugar to a nonreactive saucepan, and stir over medium heat to dissolve the sugar, then boil for 20 to 25 minutes. Add the lemon juice toward the end of cooking. When the mixture is beginning to thicken, remove the pan from the heat. Skim any foam from the surface. Stir to distribute the fruit. Pot the preserve in hot, sterilized jars. Seal. Process in a boiling-water bath, following the method on page 20. Label the jars, and store in a cool, dark place. Use within 12 months.

CHERRY SYRUP (GREEK VISINADA)

FILLS 2 1-PINT BOTTLES

2 pounds	cherries
4 cups	sugar
	juice of 1/2 lemon

Leave the sugar and cherries to macerate in a covered bowl overnight. Transfer the mixture to a nonreactive saucepan and boil for 25 minutes. Add the lemon juice and simmer for 5 minutes longer.

Remove the pan from the heat. Skim any foam from the surface. Stir to dissolve the sugar. Strain the syrup through a cheesecloth-lined funnel into hot, sterilized bottles, then cork. Process in a boiling-water bath, following the method on page 20. Label the bottles and store in a cool, dark place. Use within 12 months.

COOK'S NOTE: *You can rub the leftover cherries through a strainer, or pit them, and use the fruit with ice cream or yogurt. The syrup makes a deliciously refreshing drink when diluted with chilled sparkling mineral water, and a fabulous cocktail when combined with vodka or dark rum.*

CHERRIES IN LIQUEUR
MAKES 1 QUART
Serve three or four in a glass after dinner, as a very special treat.

2 pounds	cherries
few drops	pure almond extract
1 bottle	vodka or kirsch

Rinse and dry the cherries, keeping only perfect specimens. Remove all but 1/2 inch of the stems and pack the fruit into a 1-quart preserving jar. Sprinkle in the almond extract and fill the jar to the top with vodka, making sure all the cherries are submerged.

If necessary use the lid of a round plastic container to press down on the fruit. Seal the jar and label. Keep for at least 2 to 3 months.

COOK'S NOTE: *You can make a delicious sweetmeat for after dinner by taking a dozen cherries and patting them dry with paper towels. Melt all of a 3 1/3 ounce bar of good-quality, semisweet chocolate in a bowl set over hot water, or place the chocolate in the microwave on the appropriate setting for melting chocolate. Holding each cherry's stem with a pair of tweezers, dip it into the melted chocolate. Let any excess chocolate drip back into the bowl, then place the cherries on wax paper or baking parchment until the chocolate has set. Eat within a few hours.*

Clementines

A cross between the tangerine and the bitter, or Seville, orange, this mandarin orange ripens in fall and winter. It is useful because it is almost seedless and its thin, loose skin peels easily. In addition, it has a clean, fresh, sharp smell and flavor. The juice is fragrant and sweet but with a distinct hint of acidity, and this makes clementines suitable for marmalade. Tangerines and satsumas, and other mandarins, can be used in the same way.

■ The fruit should be deep orange, shiny-skinned, and plump, and not look dry or slightly shriveled. If using them for marmalade, thoroughly scrub and dry the skins to remove any preservatives. Some clementines are grown in California (the Pixie variety is sought after) and some are imported from Spain.

CLEMENTINE MARMALADE

FILLS 5 1-PINT JARS

There is invariably a little marmalade left over after you have filled the pots. Serve it hot over vanilla ice cream, use it to flavor a homemade ice cream, or stir it into a freshly made rice pudding.

16	clementines
1 quart	water
2	lemons
about 7 cups	sugar

Scrub the clementines well, then rinse and put them and the water in a lidded nonreactive saucepan. Halve the lemons, squeeze them, and reserve the juice. Put any pits in a cheesecloth bundle and add to the pan. Cover with a lid and simmer for 2 to 3 hours until the fruit is soft.

Remove the pan from the heat, and leave the mixture to cool overnight if this is convenient; discard the bundle of lemon pits.

Halve the clementines, and scoop the pulp and pits, if any, into a strainer set over a wide pan. Rub the pulp through the strainer, then add the cooking liquid, the sugar, and the lemon juice. Heat gently, stirring until the sugar dissolves, then boil for a few minutes.

Meanwhile, finely slice the clementine peel, then stir into the boiling sugar syrup. Continue boiling just until the marmalade reaches the setting point. Remove the pan from the heat. Skim any foam from the surface. Leave the marmalade to stand for 10 to 15 minutes to distribute the peel evenly. Fill hot, sterilized jars. Seal. Process in a boiling-water bath, following the method on page 20. Label the jars and store in a cool, dark place. Use within 12 months.

Cranberries

These tart, ruby-red berries are hardy and, because they store so well, they are sold fresh from fall to Christmas and beyond. They are normally in the shops from early November.

■ Look for shiny full berries and avoid bags that contain squashed or wizened ones. Fresh cranberries will keep, well covered, in the refrigerator for up to ten days if you first remove damaged fruit. They will keep in the freezer from one season to the next.

■ Cranberries are sourer and bitterer than any other fruit, but their high pectin content makes them a good candidate for the preserving pan. They combine well with sweeter, low-pectin fruit.

■ Long before the European settlers arrived, Native Americans preserved cranberries in pemmican, a mixture of meat and fruit that was dried to provide a useful winter food. It was Native Americans who introduced the fruit to settlers from the Old World, who quickly adopted it, together with the wild turkey. Even today, celebration meals such as Thanksgiving and Christmas would not be complete without roast turkey and cranberry sauce. But there are other preserves to be made with cranberries, including jelly and salsa.

CRANBERRY, GINGER & PORT WINE JELLY

FILLS ABOUT 5 1-PINT JARS

This firm jelly is perfect on hot biscuits or toast, and great as a relish, served with broiled and roasted poultry. You can also make a comforting cold-weather drink by stirring a spoonful or two of jelly into a tea glass of hot water.

3 cups	cranberries
4 thin slices	gingerroot, wrapped in muslin and tied
3 cups	water
1 cup	port
	sugar—*see recipe*

Put the cranberries, bundle of ginger, and water in a nonreactive saucepan and simmer until the fruit is soft. Remove the bundle of ginger. Crush the cranberries with a potato masher before spooning the pulp into a scalded jelly bag set over a nonreactive bowl, then leave to drip for a few hours, or overnight.

The next day, stir in the port and measure the volume of liquid. For every 2 cups of liquid, allow 2 cups of sugar. Put both in a saucepan and heat gently until the sugar has dissolved. Put the bundle of ginger back in the pan, then boil the mixture briskly until the setting point is reached. Remove the pan from the heat and skim any foam from the surface. Remove the ginger before pouring the jelly into hot, sterilized jars. Seal, label, and refrigerate for up to 3 months. If you wish to store the preserve for up to 12 months, at room temperature, then process in a boiling-water bath, following the instructions on page 20.

CRANBERRY SYRUP

FILLS 2 1-PINT BOTTLES

With this you can make your own cranberry-flavored cocktails, such as the Cosmopolitan.

2 pounds	cranberries, fresh or frozen
	water—*see recipe*
	sugar—*see recipe*

Put the cranberries in a nonreactive saucepan, cover with water, and simmer until the cranberries pop and are very soft. Squash them gently with a potato masher to extract as much juice and flavor as possible.

Strain the cranberries through a scalded jelly bag suspended over a large bowl, squeezing to force the liquid through, then measure the liquid. Make it up to 3 1/3 cups with water if necessary and pour it into a nonreactive saucepan. Stir in 3 cups sugar, and simmer until the sugar dissolves.

Bring to a boil then remove from the heat. Leave the syrup to cool slightly, then pour through a funnel into hot, sterilized glass bottles. Seal the bottles. Process in a boiling-water bath, following the method on page 20. Label, then store in a dark place to prevent the color from fading. Use within a year.

CRANBERRY VODKA

Keep a bottle in the freezer for instant winter cheer!

| 1 pound | cranberries, fresh or frozen |
| 1 bottle | vodka |

Put fruit and vodka in a bowl, crush with a potato masher, and leave the fruit to macerate for 2 to 3 days, covered. Strain the liquid through a cheesecloth-lined funnel into a pitcher, then decant into bottles, seal, and label.

QUICK CRANBERRY & KUMQUAT SALSA

FILLS 3 ½-PINT JARS

If you are using leftover turkey in fajitas, then this is the perfect accompaniment.

6 ounces	kumquats
1	onion, peeled and chopped
3 or 4	garlic cloves, peeled and crushed
	juice of 2 or 3 mandarin oranges
12 ounces	cranberries, fresh or frozen
¾ cup	Demerara sugar
1 or more	green chilies, seeded and finely chopped
	salt and pepper

Halve the kumquats, discard the seeds, and quarter the fruit. Put the kumquats, onion, garlic, cranberries, and orange juice in a nonreactive saucepan, half cover and simmer until the cranberries pop. Stir in the sugar and chilies, then when the sugar dissolves, bring to a boil. Boil until the mixture thickens.

Remove the pan from the heat. Spoon the salsa into sterilized hot jars, then seal. Leave to cool completely and refrigerate. For a longer storage period, process the jars in a boiling-water bath, following the method on page 20. Label, then put in a cool, dark place. Use within 12 months.

SPICED CRANBERRY SAUCE

FILLS 2 ½-PINT JARS

This is the cranberry sauce I make every year, in late November, to accompany everything from the Thanksgiving turkey to the New Year cold table.

12 ounces	cranberries, fresh or frozen
	juice and zest of 2 oranges
4	star anise pods
1³/4 cups	sugar

Put the cranberries, orange juice and zest, and star anise in a nonreactive saucepan, partially cover the pan with its lid, and cook gently until the cranberries pop. Stir in the sugar and, when it dissolves, boil the mixture until it reaches the setting point, about 10 to 15 minutes at the most.

Remove the pan from the heat. Spoon the preserve into hot, sterilized jars, then seal. Process the jars in a boiling-water bath, following the method on page 20. Label. This sauce can be used immediately and will keep in the refrigerator for 8 to 12 weeks. To store longer, put in a cool, dark place. Use within 12 months.

Currants

These delicious soft berry fruits grow in temperate climates, and are in season in summer. Black and red currants are the most widely available, although a rare white currant, an albino strain of the red, can sometimes be found.

■ To detach the berries from the stems ready for use, simply run a fork down the length of the stem held over a bowl.

■ Red and black currants are marvelous for jams and jellies because they are rich in pectin, and, because of this, need a relatively short cooking time, which helps to retain their fresh flavor.

■ A good jelly to accompany meat and game dishes is made with black currants and fresh mint leaves. Black currant syrups and cordials are popular winter remedies against colds and coughs because they are rich in vitamin C.

BLACK CURRANT SYRUP

FILLS 3 1-PINT BOTTLES

A spoonful or two in a glass of hot water makes a soothing drink in winter and, when diluted with chilled sparkling water, refreshes in summer.

2 pounds	black currants
1 cup	water
4 cups	sugar

Put the fruit and water in a nonreactive saucepan and cook until the fruit is soft, then mash with a potato masher to extract as much juice and flavor as possible. Strain the fruit through a scalded cheesecloth-lined strainer over a saucepan. Add the sugar, stirring, bring to a boil and remove from the heat. Decant into hot, sterilized bottles, then cork. Process the bottles in a boiling-water bath, following the method on page 20. Label. Store in a cool, dark place. Use within 12 months.

BLACK CURRANT & MINT JELLY

FILLS 5 ½-PINT JARS

Perfect on toast, black currant jelly makes a surprisingly good filling for chocolate cakes, as well as an accompaniment to meat and game dishes.

2 pounds	black currants
bunch	fresh mint leaves—about 2 ounces
2½ cups	water
	sugar—*see recipe*

Put the fruit, most of the mint leaves and the stems, and water in a nonreactive saucepan and simmer until the fruit is soft. Remove the pan from the heat. Crush the fruit with a potato masher, then spoon it into a scalded jelly bag over a bowl and leave it to drip, without squeezing or forcing, for several hours or overnight.

The next day, measure the juice. For each 2 cups juice, add 2 cups sugar. Put both in a saucepan and heat gently until the sugar dissolves. Add the remaining mint leaves, then boil briskly without stirring, until the setting point is reached. Remove the pan from the heat and remove the mint leaves before pouring the jelly into hot, sterilized jars. Seal. Process the jars in a boiling-water bath, following the method on page 20. Label. Store in a cool, dark place. Use within 12 months.

CASSIS

FILLS 3 1-PINT BOTTLES

Make your own version of the French black currant liqueur, and you will always have on hand the main ingredient of a Kir, or vin blanc cassis, a simple and delicious aperitif. Pour the cassis over raspberry sorbet for a truly fabulous taste sensation.

2 pounds	black currants
1 cup	water
2 cups	sugar
1 bottle	vodka

Put the fruit and water in a nonreactive saucepan and cook until the fruit is soft, then mash with a potato masher to extract as much juice and flavor as possible. Strain the fruit through a scalded cheesecloth-lined strainer over another saucepan.

Add the sugar, stirring until it dissolves, then bring to a boil and remove from the heat. Leave to cool completely, then stir in the vodka. Decant into bottles, cork, and label.

RED CURRANT, CIDER & PEPPER JELLY

FILLS 2 ½-PINT JARS

This is a savory jelly, to serve with broiled, barbecued, and roasted meats, especially lamb and game. But also try it brushed over a salmon fillet, just before broiling.

1 pound	red currants
1 cup	water
1 teaspoon *each*	black, green, and pink peppercorns
½ cup	cider vinegar
	sugar—*see recipe*

Put the fruit, water, and ½ teaspoon of each peppercorn in a nonreactive saucepan and simmer until the fruit is soft. Crush it with a potato masher, then spoon it into a scalded jelly bag over a bowl or large pitcher and let it drip without squeezing or forcing, for several hours, or overnight if possible.

The next day, measure the juice, then add the vinegar and the remaining peppercorns. For each 2 cups liquid, add 2 cups sugar. Put both in a nonreactive sauce pan and heat until the sugar dissolves, then bring to a boil. Boil until the setting point is reached.

Remove the pan from the heat. Skim any foam from the surface. Ladle the jelly into hot, sterilized jars. Seal. Process the jars in a boiling-water bath, following the method on page 20. Label. Store in a cool, dark place. Use within 12 months.

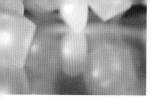
Dates

Grown in warm Mediterranean climates, the date, with its luscious sweetness, has long been a symbol of hospitality. At about seventy per cent, the carbohydrate content of dates is higher than in any other fruit. The date seed is inedible, and should be removed before simmering. To remove it, split the date lengthwise and ease the seed out with the point of a knife.

DATE JAM

FILLS 3 ½-PINT JARS

Date jam is a lovely winter preserve, especially for tartlettes. I also use the date jam as a purée to accompany broiled duck breasts, or as a glaze for roast duck or pork. The date jam is also delicious served with yogurt, ice cream, crêpes and coeurs à la crème, the small French cream–cheese hearts.

1 pound	good-quality, ripe, whole dates, pitted and chopped
	grated zest and juice of 1 lemon
3/4 cup + 2 tblsp	water
1 1/4 cups	sugar
1 to 2 teaspoons	fennel seeds or aniseed
2 tablespoons	sesame seeds, lightly toasted *(optional)*
2 tablespoons	shelled walnuts, chopped *(optional)*
2 tablespoons	slivered almonds, lightly toasted
2 teaspoons	rosewater or orange flower water

Put the dates, lemon zest and juice, water, sugar, and fennel seed or aniseed in a nonreactive saucepan and simmer gently, stirring until the sugar dissolves and the mixture thickens slightly.

Remove the pan from the heat. Rub the date mixture through a plastic or nylon strainer, then add the nuts, or seeds, if using, and stir in the flower water. Spoon the jam into small, sterilized jars, then seal and label for presents, or keep in an airtight container in the refrigerator.

DATE, BANANA & TAMARIND CHUTNEY

FILLS 4 1/2-PINT JARS

This is a delicious, subtle, and mellow chutney, to be served not only with Asian food, but also with broiled and grilled meat, and poultry. It is perfect, too, with cheddar or other hard cheese.

1 cup	dates, pitted and chopped
1	onion, peeled, quartered, and thinly sliced
6	bananas, peeled and sliced
1/2 cup	distilled vinegar
large 3/4 cup	Demerara or soft, light brown sugar
2 ounces	tamarind pulp, strained
2 tablespoons	peeled and grated, or finely chopped, fresh gingerroot
1 teaspoon	mild or medium curry paste

Put the bananas, onion, dates, and vinegar in a nonreactive saucepan and simmer until the onion is soft. Add the remaining ingredients and simmer until the mixture is a rich brown color, with a slightly jammy consistency; this will take 20 to 30 minutes.

Remove the pan from the heat. Skim any foam from the surface. Pot the chutney in hot, sterilized jars, then seal. Process the jars in a boiling-water bath, following the method on page 20. Label. Store in a cool, dark place. Use within 12 months.

COOK'S NOTE: *Tamarind pulp is a delicate souring agent, taken from the seedpod of the magnificent tamarind tree, and is widely used in Asian cooking. It is available from specialist food stores and Asian food stores and markets.*

Figs

Rare and expensive outside the Mediterranean climate zone, which includes California, the fig is usually eaten as a dessert. But if available in abundance, they can be made into a heavenly jam.

Look for firm, unblemished fruit that just yields when you hold it in your hand without pressing. The skin of a perfectly ripe fruit is velvety and soft, rather taut and satiny. It can be a number of colors from pale green and golden yellow to deep purple.

FRESH FIG JAM

FILLS 6 ½-PINT JARS

This is a delicious jam, looking and tasting as fresh and bright as strawberry jam. It is essential to use commercial pectin as figs contain little or no natural pectin.

2 pounds	ripe purple figs
1 cup	water
4 cups	sugar
4 teaspoons	liquid pectin

Peel and quarter the figs, put them in a bowl, and cover them with the sugar. Leave overnight. Simmer the fig skins in a small saucepan with the water for about 15 minutes, then strain them and reserve the lovely red juice.

Next day, combine the fruit, pectin, and sugar with the fig juice in a nonreactive saucepan, and simmer gently until the sugar dissolves. Follow the instructions that come with the pectin, and boil until the setting point is reached, which may be as little as 4 minutes. Remove the pan from the heat. Skim any foam from the surface, then pot the jam in hot, sterilized jars. Seal. Process in a boiling-water bath, following the method on page 20. Label. Store in a cool, dark place. Use within 12 months.

Gooseberries

The tart green gooseberries are available from late spring, lasting throughout summer, joined toward the middle of the season by large yellow and red dessert gooseberries. American-grown gooseberries run from May to August. New Zealand-grown supplies go from October through June, depending on the variety, but most arrive in November, December, and January.

Gooseberries are a good source of dietary fiber and rich in pectin, which makes them an ideal fruit for jams, chutneys, and jellies. I make them into jelly; I love its pale pink-gold color.

When simmering the fruit for jelly-making there isn't any need to top and tail, but for any preserve recipe that requires the whole berry, use a sharp knife or scissors to trim them. The juice that drips through the scalded jelly bag suspended over a bowl without squeezing or forcing has a tartness that makes it an interesting substitute for lemon or lime juice. I use it in salad dressings, marinades, and fish sauces.

GOOSEBERRY CHUTNEY

FILLS 8 ½-PINT JARS

Serve this with crusty bread and a fine artisan cheese, or other mature cheese.

4 pounds	gooseberries, topped and tailed
2	tart apples, such as Granny Smith, peeled, cored, and sliced
1	large mild onion, peeled and chopped
2½ cups	spiced vinegar—*see page 15*
4 cups	soft brown or Demerara sugar
1 teaspoon	freshly ground black pepper, cinnamon, cardamom, and cloves
3½ cups	raisins
	salt to taste

Cook the gooseberries, apples, and onion in a heavy, nonreactive saucepan, adding a few tablespoons water to stop the mixture sticking. When the onions are soft, add the vinegar and sugar, stirring until it dissolves. Add the remaining ingredients then simmer, stirring, until thick. Remove the pan from the heat. Pot the chutney in hot, sterilized jars and seal. Process in a boiling-water bath, following the method on page 20. Label. Store in a cool, dark place for 2 months before using. Use within 12 months.

GOOSEBERRY JAM

FILLS 10 ½-PINT JARS

Hot buttered toast is the perfect companion for this jam, which is easy to make.

3 pounds	gooseberries, tails and stems snipped, rinsed
2 cups	water
8 cups	sugar

Put the gooseberries in a nonreactive saucepan with the water. Simmer until the fruit is tender, then stir in the sugar until it dissolves. Bring to a boil and boil the mixture rapidly until the setting point is reached. Remove the pan from the heat. Skim any foam from the surface. Pot the jam in hot, sterilized jars, then seal. Process in a boiling-water bath, following the method on page 20. Label. Store in a cool, dark place. Use within 12 months.

GOOSEBERRY JELLY WITH SAUVIGNON BLANC

FILLS 4 14-OUNCE JARS

Hints of gooseberry are often found in wines made with the sauvignon blanc grape. Here, I combine the two in a jelly with intriguing flavors. It is excellent for glazing fruit tarts.

3 pounds	gooseberries, rinsed
	sauvignon blanc wine—*see recipe*
	sugar—*see recipe*

Put the gooseberries in a nonreactive saucepan. Add enough wine to cover the gooseberries by an inch or so and simmer until the gooseberries are soft. Mash the fruit to extract as much juice and pectin as possible. Strain through a scalded jelly bag suspended over a bowl without squeezing or forcing for several hours or overnight.

The next day, measure the liquid, and put it in a nonreactive saucepan, then stir in an equal amount of sugar. Heat the mixture, stirring until the sugar dissolves, then bring to a boil. Boil until the setting point is reached. Remove the pan from the heat. Skim any foam from the surface. Pot the jelly in hot, sterilized jars, then seal. Process in a boiling-water bath, following the method on page 20. Label. Store in a cool, dark place. Use within 12 months.

Grapes

With very few exceptions, grapes grown expressly for wine-making do not appear in stores. Wine grapes are smaller, sharper tasting, and have tougher skins than those grown for the table. Some varieties, however—such as the Chasselas and the Muscat—are cultivated both for the table and for wine-making. These two are particularly good in jellies. For the chutney, any of the standard table varieties can be used, red, black, or green, and select seedless if they are available.

QUICK & EASY GRAPE & GINGER CHUTNEY

FILLS 5 ½-PINT JARS

This is an excellent accompaniment to curries, but is also good on cheese sandwiches.

2½ cups	light brown, or Demerara sugar
2 cups	wine vinegar—*see recipe*
2	garlic cloves, peeled and crushed
2	shallots, peeled and chopped
5 to 6 tablespoons	gingerroot, peeled and grated
2 pounds	seedless red, black, or green grapes
3 to 4 ounces *each*	raisins and sultanas
2	tart apples, such as Granny Smith, peeled, cored, and grated
1 or 2	dried chilies, seeds removed, and crumbled
	salt to taste

If using green grapes, use white wine vinegar, otherwise use red wine vinegar. Warm the sugar and vinegar in a nonreactive saucepan, stirring until the sugar dissolves, then boil without stirring until you have a thin syrup, about 10 minutes.

Stir in the remaining ingredients except the salt, bring to a boil, then lower the heat, and simmer until the mixture is soft and jammy in consistency. Stir in the salt. Remove the pan from the heat. Skim any foam from the surface. Pot the chutney in hot, sterilized jars, then seal. Process the jars in a boiling-water bath, following the method on page 20. Label. Store in a cool, dark place for at least 2 months before using. Use within 12 months.

DAMASK ROSE & BLACK MUSCAT GRAPE JELLY

FILLS 4 ½-PINT JARS

This is a gorgeous preserve, to be made whenever you are lucky enough to have access to unsprayed scented roses. These will almost certainly be from a flower garden, not a florist. I suggest small jars because this jam is so special, you will want some for yourself and some to give away.

1 or 2	large tart green apples such as Granny Smith
1 large bunch	black muscat grapes, stems removed
	sugar—*see recipe*
2 cups or more	dark red, scented, unsprayed rose petals, loosely packed and measured in a measuring pitcher
1 tablespoon	rosewater, if necessary

Wash the apples, cut them into chunks, without peeling or coring, and put them into a nonreactive saucepan with enough water to cover them by 1 inch or so. Simmer until the apples are almost soft, then add the grapes and continue simmering until they are soft. Mash the fruit to extract as much juice and pectin as possible. Strain the fruit through a scalded jelly bag suspended over a bowl, without squeezing or forcing, for several hours or overnight.

The next day, measure the liquid and put it in the washed saucepan. Measure an equal amount of sugar. Pound half the rose petals in a small quantity of the sugar, then add to the juice with the rest of the sugar. Heat the liquid gently, stirring until the sugar dissolves, then add the remaining rose petals, and bring the syrup to a boil. Taste and add the rosewater if you think it is necessary. Boil fast until the setting point is reached. Remove the pan from the heat. Skim any foam from the surface. Pot the jelly in small, hot, sterilized jam jars, then seal. Process the jars in a boiling-water bath, following the method on page 20. Label. Store in a cool, dark place. Use within 12 months.

Grapefruit

A large, yellow-skinned, tart member of the citrus family, grapefruit is available most of the year. First brought to Florida from the Bahamas in 1820 by a French nobleman, the fruit flourished to such an extent that Florida now produces 75 percent of the American grapefruit crop, followed by Texas, California, and Arizona. Indian River grapefruit are the most sought after, and they are available with white and pink flesh, Burgundy being a favorite variety. It has a long growing season, from November to July. Rio Red, Ruby Red, and Star Red are, as their names suggest, red-fleshed varieties.

Choose fruit that is heavy for its size—a sign of juiciness—with plump skin and the distinctive, sharp, citrus aroma.

Grapefruit marmalade is one of the best versions of this breakfast favorite, and the crystallized peel is elegant to serve with after-dinner coffee.

GRAPEFRUIT & GINGER MARMALADE

FILLS 3 1-PINT JARS

This marmalade is a delight for a leisurely breakfast.

2 to 3	large grapefruits
thumb-size piece	fresh gingerroot, peeled, sliced, and cut into shreds
2¹/2 cups	water
4 cups	sugar

Scrub the fruit well, then rinse, and put in a nonreactive saucepan with the water and ginger. Cover and simmer for 2 hours or until soft. Remove the pan from the heat, and leave the grapefruit to cool, overnight.

The next day, halve the fruit, scoop the pulp and seeds into a strainer, set over a wide pan, then rub the pulp into a nonreactive saucepan. Add the cooking liquid and the sugar, and heat gently until the sugar dissolves. Bring the mixture to a boil then continue boiling for a few minutes.

Meanwhile, finely slice the grapefruit peel, or process for a few seconds in the food processor. Stir this into the boiling sugar syrup and continue boiling just until the marmalade reaches the setting point.

Remove the pan from the heat. Skim any foam from the surface, and leave to stand for 5 minutes to distribute the peel evenly. Pot the marmalade in hot, sterilized jars, then seal. Process in a boiling-water bath, following the method on page 20. Label. Store in a cool, dark place. Use within 12 months.

COOK'S NOTE: *For extra flavor, you can add a generous splash of rum to the marmalade just before potting.*

CRYSTALLIZED GRAPEFRUIT PEEL

Crystallized peel makes an excellent present, especially if you dip them in good-quality melted chocolate containing at least 70 percent cocoa solids. Pink-fleshed grapefruit produces a pretty pale orange peel when crystallized; the peel of the yellow-fleshed fruit remains yellow.

2	grapefruits, squeezed
	water—*see recipe*
1¹/4 cups	sugar

Discard the membranes and cut the grapefruit skins into neat strips. Put them in a nonreactive saucepan and cover with water, bring to a boil, and simmer until the peel is tender and translucent. Drain and rinse the peels, then return them to the pan with 3/4 cup water and 1 cup sugar. Stir and simmer until the sugar dissolves, then continue to simmer, stirring in the remaining sugar after about 10 minutes.

When the syrup has almost been absorbed and becomes sticky to the touch, but before it reaches the brittle, crack stage, transfer the pieces of peel to wire racks. Leave them to dry, overnight if possible, then roll them in sugar and store in an airtight box. They will keep for 2 to 3 weeks.

GRAPEFRUIT CURD

FILLS 4 ½-PINT JARS

The curd is delicious served with vanilla ice cream, or as a filling for tartlettes.

4	grapefruits with good skins
6	large eggs, lightly beaten
2 sticks	unsalted butter, cut into small cubes
2 cups	sugar

Grate the zest and squeeze the juice from the grapefruit then put them in the top of a double saucepan over low heat. Add the eggs, butter, and sugar and stir until the sugar dissolves. Continue simmering and stirring until the mixture thickens, about 30 minutes (you can use an electric stick blender and the process will only take a few minutes).

Remove the pan from the heat. Skim any foam from the surface. Pot the curd in small, sterilized jars and cover immediately. Label, refrigerate, and use within 3 to 4 weeks. Alternatively, freeze the mixture in small containers for up to 2 months.

COOK'S NOTE: *This recipe uses uncooked eggs.*

Guavas

The best guavas are small, soft-skinned, fragrant, pale yellow, pear-shaped fruit. Once cut open, the fruit yields pink, softly grainy flesh, with flat crunchy seeds. The smaller and pinker they are, the more flavor they have; use these for preserves. The more available guavas are larger, paler, with a creamy flesh, and less scented. Fully ripe guavas have yellow skin and a warm fragrance.

Guavas, available all year, except in spring, come from Central and Southern America, the Caribbean, and Thailand. They are fragile, so handle them with care and use soon after buying.

Colombia and Brazil produce delicious guava specialties, from a soft clear jelly to a sweetmeat thick enough to slice. It is worth making both jelly and paste, as the leftover pulp from the jelly recipes can be used for the paste.

GUAVA JELLY

FILLS 3 ½-PINT JARS

In Latin America, cream cheese and guava preserve is a popular filling for breakfast pastries, and is just as delicious spread on hot toast or biscuits.

2 pounds	fresh guavas, peeled and halved
1 cup	water
	sugar—*see recipe*
	juice of 2 lemons
5 teaspoons	liquid or powdered pectin

Put the guavas in a nonreactive saucepan with the water and simmer until the fruit is soft. Mash the fruit to extract as much juice as possible. Drip the pulp through a scalded jelly bag suspended over a bowl, without squeezing or forcing, overnight.

The next day, measure the liquid, adding the lemon juice, and put the liquids in a nonreactive saucepan. For each 2 cups liquid, stir in 1½ cups sugar and the pectin, and stir until the sugar dissolves. Then bring to a boil and boil until the setting point is reached.

Remove the pan from the heat. Skim any foam from the surface. Pour the jelly into hot, sterilized jars, then seal. Process in a boiling-water bath, following the method on page 20. Label. Store in a cool place. Use within 12 months.

GUAVA PASTE (DULCE DE GUAYABA)

FILLS 3 ½-PINT JARS

Serve with a slice of ricotta or other cheese. Also try it with blue cheese for a taste revelation.

2 cups	guava pulp, drained weight
1½ cups	sugar
	juice of 1 lemon

Rub the pulp from the previous recipe through a plastic strainer. Put the guava puree in a nonreactive saucepan with the sugar and lemon juice over medium heat, stirring until the sugar dissolves. Bring to a boil, lower the heat, and simmer until you can draw a spoon through the mix and the mix does not close together.

Remove the pan from the heat. Skim any foam from the surface. Pour the fruit puree into a shallow greased pan and leave until set and cool. Turn out, cut into squares or wedges, wrap in wax paper, and store in the refrigerator in an airtight box, where it will keep for several weeks.

GUAVA PRESERVE

FILLS 3 ½-PINT JARS

Firmer and denser than the jelly but softer than the paste, guava preserve makes a delicious filling for cakes, tarts, and pastries, with or without cream or cream cheese.

1 pound	fresh guavas, peeled and halved
	water—*see recipe*
	juice of 1 lemon
2 cups	sugar
1 tablespoon	liquid or powdered pectin

Scoop out the seeds from the guavas and put them in a saucepan with the skins and about ¾ cup water. Simmer for 20 to 30 minutes, then strain the liquid through a cheesecloth-lined nylon strainer into a larger nonreactive saucepan.

Add the guavas, sliced or cut into chunks, and simmer until just soft. Add the sugar, pectin, and lemon juice, stirring to dissolve the sugar, then bring to a boil, without stirring, until the setting point is reached.

Remove the pan from the heat. Skim any foam from the surface. Spoon the preserve into small, hot, sterilized jars, then seal. Process the jars in a boiling-water bath, following the method on page 20. Label. Store in a cool, dark place. Use within 12 months.

Kiwifruit *(also known as Chinese Gooseberry)*

Once considered a rare and exotic fruit from China, the kiwifruit, because it is now grown in both the northern and southern hemispheres, is generally available all year around. The fruit is grown extensively in California, with a long growing season from October to May, and stands up well to lengthy cold storage, so even when there is not much fruit about, one can rely on finding kiwis on the supermarket shelves.

The bright green flesh and tiny black seeds, encased in a furry brown skin, are edible. The sweet flavor is more than matched by a high degree of acidity, and it is not surprising to learn that each fresh fruit contains more than the daily requirement of vitamin C for an adult. The kiwi is so acidic that it cannot be used in recipes calling for aspic or gelatin, as the amino acids dissolve these. Because of its acidity, I have always found the kiwifruit more suited to pickles and chutneys than jams. I like to make an uncooked fresh kiwi salsa, using green chilies and scallions with the fruit, together with some lime zest and juice and chopped cilantro, but it also makes excellent ketchup and chutney.

KIWI & JALAPENO KETCHUP

FILLS 1 1-PINT BOTTLE

The ketchup is a very versatile condiment, excellent with broiled or barbecued poultry or fish, and also a useful ingredient to brush on before broiling. It is very good, too, as an accompaniment to smoked fish and meats.

6	shallots, peeled and chopped
6	moderately ripe kiwifruit, peeled and diced
1 or 2	jalapeño peppers, halved, seeded, and thinly sliced
1/2 teaspoon *each*	ground cumin, cilantro, and cloves
1 cup	vinegar—cider, white wine, or distilled
1 cup	sugar

Simmer the shallots in the water in a nonreactive saucepan until almost tender, then add the kiwifruit flesh, the jalapeño, and the spices and continue simmering for 30 minutes or so. Add the vinegar and sugar, stirring to dissolve the sugar, and simmer for about 15 minutes longer or until the mixture thickens.

Remove the pan from the heat. Skim any foam from the surface. When the mixture cools, strain or blend it until smooth. Store it in the refrigerator in squeezy bottles with nozzles. This way, if a simple dollop will not suffice, you can splash and swirl the ketchup on the plate. If you are planning to store the ketchup at room temperature, process in a boiling-water bath following the method on page 20. Label. Use within 12 months.

COOK'S NOTE: *In many of my pickle and chutney recipes I recommend one of the raw or unrefined sugars, but in this case I recommend white sugar, otherwise the kiwifruit cooks to a less-than-appetizing khaki color. Indeed, it is one of the few recipes where I would consider using a dash of food coloring to keep a true green.*

KIWI CHUTNEY

FILLS 4 1-PINT JARS

This is a classic chutney, as at home with Indian curries as with a platter of cheese and crusty bread.

2	tart apples, such as a Granny Smith
9	large kiwifruit, peeled and diced
3	green chilies, thinly sliced
2 tablespoons	grated fresh peeled gingerroot
	juice and grated zest of 2 limes or lemons
2½ cups	sugar
2½ cups	white wine or cider vinegar
	salt to taste

Peel, core, and dice the apple very small. Put it in a nonreactive saucepan with a little water and simmer until almost soft. Add the kiwis, chilies, and ginger, as well as the citrus juice and zest, sugar, and vinegar, stirring the sugar. Bring to a boil, then reduce the heat and simmer until the mixture thickens, 25 to 30 minutes.

Remove the pan from the heat. Skim any foam from the surface. Pot the chutney in hot, sterilized jars, then seal. Process the jars in a boiling-water bath, following the method on page 20. Label. Store for at least 2 months in a cool, dark place before opening, but it also very good to eat within a few days of making. Use within 12 months.

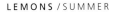

Lemons

Choose lemons that feel heavy for their size. Small, thin-skinned ones will be juicier, and the larger, knobbly ones will have more peel and pith in proportion to flesh. The latter are perfect for candying and preserving, as it is the essential oils in the skin that you want to preserve, as much as the juice.

The fruit we buy in the stores keeps well because it has been treated to preserve it from rot and the other evils that attack fresh fruit—so scrub them well if you intend to use the skin. Increasingly, unwaxed lemons, often organically grown, are available, and these are what I use for lemon curd and marmalade. Storing them in a plastic bag or box in the refrigerator will help preserve their moisture content better than leaving them in a bowl in the kitchen.

The citron is a large, lemon-shaped fruit of the citrus family, up to 8 inches in length. The peel, rough-textured and greenish to golden yellow, and the pith are the important elements as it is a fruit used solely for candying, crystallizing, or otherwise preserving. The pulp is very sour. Very occasionally it is available commercially, and it is worth buying to make either lemon curd or marmalade. Its natural habitat is the Amalfi coast of southern Italy, where it is used to make the liqueur limoncello.

LEMON CURD

FILLS 4 ½-PINT JARS

As well as being delicious on toasted muffins, the curd can be used as a filling for tarts. It can also be spooned into baked pastry cases and put in the oven, at 350°F for 5 minutes. Serve warm, dusted with confectioners' sugar.

4	large lemons with good skins
2	large egg yolks, plus 4 whole large eggs, lightly beaten
1¾ sticks	unsalted butter, cut into small cubes
1½ cups	sugar

Grate the zest and squeeze the juice from the lemons, and put in the top of a double boiler, or in a stainless-steel saucepan set inside a larger saucepan half filled with simmering water. Add the eggs, butter, and sugar and stir until the sugar dissolves. Continue simmering and stirring until the mixture thickens. Remove the pan from the heat. Skim any foam from the surface. Spoon the curd into warm, sterilized jars, cover, then seal immediately. Label, leave to cool completely, then refrigerate. Use within 4 to 6 weeks.

Making the curd the traditional way, in a double boiler or a china bowl set over a saucepan of water and stirring with a wooden spoon, can take 45 minutes or so. In a stainless steel saucepan and beating with an electric stick blender the whole process takes about 10 minutes.

NOTE: *This contains raw eggs.*

COOK'S NOTE: *One of the best ice creams I have ever tasted is made by mixing a pot of lemon curd with a carton of cream and freezing the mixture. Before it is completely frozen, stir the mixture thoroughly, then carefully fold in broken meringues and finish the freezing in the freezer, not in the ice cream machine, or it will churn the meringue to crumbs. You want to retain enough texture for the ice cream to crunch when you eat it, for then you have lemon meringue ice cream.*

LIMONCELLO

FILLS 3 1-QUART BOTTLES

Excellent when you want to simmer something in an exotic sauce and delicious when splashed on ice cream, limoncello is also heavenly in a Martini-style cocktail. I keep a bottle in the freezer to serve as a digestif after a special meal.

6 to 8	unwaxed lemons
1 quart bottle	vodka
4 cups	sugar

Carefully peel the lemon skins without removing any white pith, which will make the liqueur bitter. Put the peel in a glass pitcher or decanter, of at least 1-quart capacity, and fill to the top with vodka. Cover the top with plastic wrap and keep on a sunny windowsill for 3 to 4 weeks.

Once you have sealed the container of vodka and zest, halve and squeeze the lemons and make up the amount of juice to 1 quart with water. Put this liquid in a nonreactive saucepan with the sugar and simmer, stirring until the sugar dissolves. Bring to a boil, then remove the pan from the heat and store the lemon syrup until the vodka and lemon peel have finished infusing. Strain the syrup into a large pitcher, then strain in the flavored vodka. Mix together well, then pour the pale yellow liquid, which will be cloudy, not clear, through a funnel into sterilized bottles. Then seal with cork, or screw top, and label. It will keep for 12 months in a cool, dry place, longer if kept in the freezer.

COOK'S NOTE: *I use the vodka-soaked lemon zest in baking. First, I let the zest dry out, then I grind it with sugar, and use that as some, or all of, the sugar required in cake or cookie recipes.*

PICKLED SPICED LEMONS

FILLS 3 1-PINT JARS

An important ingredient in Moroccan and Middle Eastern cooking, especially in tagines, soups, and stews, pickled lemons are easy to make and keep very well. A little chopped pickled lemon also makes a very good relish for smoked meats and fish.

12	small lemons
	water—*see recipe*
	salt—*see recipe*
1 teaspoon	cumin seeds
1 teaspoon	cilantro seeds
1 teaspoon	black peppercorns
seeds from 8	green cardamom pods
6	cloves
	olive oil

Put the lemons in a nonreactive saucepan and pour sufficient boiling water over to cover. Simmer for 3 to 4 minutes, then drain the lemons in a colander over the sink. Rinse the lemons under cold water until cool enough to handle and then quarter them and pack them into hot, sterilized preserving jars.

Dissolve 1/2 cup salt in 1 quart water in a nonreactive saucepan, and bring it to a boil. Distribute the spices among the jars of lemons, pour the boiling brine over, to within 1/2 inch of the rim of the jar, and make sure there are not any air bubbles. Pour enough olive oil into each jar to float on top of the brine and form a seal. Screw on the sterilized lids, label, and keep in a cool, dry place for at least 2 to 3 months before using.

Limes

The main supplies of this small green citrus fruit come from Florida, the Caribbean, and Brazil. Unlike its cousin the lemon, it grows in tropical and subtropical climates, and is associated with many dishes of, for example, India and Southeast Asia, where it also grows readily, and is used all of the time in recipes.

As with all citrus, look for fruit that is heavy for its size with plump, unblemished skin. The thin-skinned fruit will have more juice; thicker-fleshed fruit is better if you need the zest. The lemon curd recipe on page 71 can also be used to make lime curd.

LIME PICKLE

FILLS 2 ½-PINT JARS

For those who love the occasional curry, here is the perfect accompaniment, a sharp lime pickle, delicious eaten in tiny bites with tandoori chicken. I developed the recipe from an old one dating back to the days of the British Raj. Do not attempt it with oranges, even bitter oranges, nor with thick-skinned lemons. The flavor you are after is hot and sour, not hot, sour, and bitter. (Bitterness is the flavor you get from the pith of thick-skinned citrus fruit.)

1 pound	limes
2 tablespoons	sea salt
8	garlic cloves, peeled
1 thumb-size piece	fresh gingerroot, peeled, roughly diced
4 or 5	dried hot chilies
2/3 cup	wine or cider vinegar
2 tablespoons	cumin seeds
1 tablespoon	cilantro seeds
2 tablespoons	mustard seeds
seeds of 8	green cardamom pods
1¼ cups	canola, peanut, or sunflower oil

Cut the fruit into wedges, then again across in 2 or 3 pieces. Cover with salt and leave in a nonreactive bowl for 2 hours. Drain and press the limes well. In a food processor or mortar, pound the garlic, ginger, and chilies to a paste with ¼ cup of

the vinegar. Grind the spices to a powder. (You can use ground spices, but I think it is best to grind them yourself, for a fresher flavor, though I understand this is not always possible.)

Heat the oil in a nonreactive saucepan and simmer the spices in it for 10 minutes over low heat, stirring constantly. Then add the garlic, ginger, and chili paste and stir for 10 minutes longer. Add the drained citrus together with the remaining vinegar, and simmer until the peel softens considerably and everything else has cooked to a curry-like consistency. This can take a couple of hours over very low heat and you will need to stir from time to time.

Remove the pan from the heat. Skim any foam from the surface. Pot the pickle in hot, sterilized jars, then seal. Process the jars in a boiling-water bath following the method on page 20. Label. Store in a cool, dry place for 2 months at least to mature the pickle. Use within 2 years.

COOK'S NOTE: *It is a good idea to have all the windows open when you make the pickle, otherwise your kitchen will smell like a pickle factory. Your hair and clothes certainly will. Given the time involved, it is probably worth doubling and tripling quantities, as the pickle keeps well, and is a perfect present for curry aficionados.*

Loganberries

Judge Logan, in whose Californian garden the first plant was discovered accidentally 100 years ago, gave his name to this juicy fruit, said to be a cross between his own raspberries and wild blackberries growing on the other side of his fence.

More hybrids have appeared. Boysenberries were developed from the strawberry, raspberry, dewberry, and loganberry, and most closely resemble plump blackberries, with similar glossy drupelets. Youngberries are hybrids of the dewberry and the loganberry and are not, as yet, widely cultivated.

When choosing any of these berries, look for sound, firm, dry, fully ripe specimens. The fruit grows high off the ground so they should not be dirty, and do not require washing, which drains them of flavor. Remove squashed or moldy fruit you find, along with any stems or leaves.

The fruit is larger, softer, and darker red than the raspberry and is slightly more acidic. Do not keep them longer than 24 hours before using because their fragrance and flavor soon disappear.

LOGANBERRY & PINOT NOIR JELLY

FILLS 4 ½ PINT JARS

Delicious as a filling for crêpes, or a topping for hotcakes.

2 pounds	loganberries
1 cup	pinot noir wine
	sugar—*see recipe*
	juice of 1 lemon
2 tablespoons	powdered pectin

Rinse, then hull the fruit and put in a nonreactive saucepan with the wine. Simmer until soft, then crush with a potato masher. Spoon the pulp into a scalded jelly bag, suspended over a bowl, and leave the fruit to drip for several hours. Measure the liquid and allow 2 cups sugar to 1 pint liquid. Put both in a saucepan, together with the lemon juice and pectin, stirring well. Heat until the sugar has dissolved, then boil briskly until the setting point is reached. Remove the pan from the heat. Skim any foam from the surface. Pot the jelly in small, hot, sterilized jars. Seal. Process in a boiling-water bath following the method on page 20. Label the jars. Store in a cool, dark place and use within 12 months.

LOGANBERRY JAM

FILLS 4 1-PINT JARS

Another quintessential treat with warm biscuits or hot buttered toast, loganberry jam also makes a good filling for a layer cake. And it is delicious stirred into a pot of plain yogurt for breakfast or midday snack.

3 pounds	loganberries
6 cups	sugar
2 tablespoons	powdered or liquid pectin

Put the fruit in a nonreactive saucepan and simmer gently until the juices begin to run and the fruit to break up. Stir in the sugar, and pectin and when the sugar dissolves, boil briskly until the setting point is reached. Remove the pan from the heat. Skim any foam from the surface. Pot the jam in hot, sterilized jars, then seal. Process the jars in a boiling-water bath following the method on page 20. Label. Store in a cool, dry place for at least 2 months to mature. Use within 12 months.

LOGANBERRY VINEGAR

FILLS 2 ½-PINT BOTTLES

Slightly overripe fruit can be crushed and steeped in wine vinegar to make an excellent fruit vinegar for simmering. For example, use to deglaze the pan when cooking duck breasts or noisettes of venison.

1 pound	loganberries
2 cups	red wine vinegar
½ cup	sugar

Put the fruit in a nonreactive bowl with the sugar and pour the vinegar over. Cover and leave to steep for 48 hours. Crush the fruit with a potato masher, then strain through cheesecloth or a very fine strainer into a pitcher. Decant into sterilized bottles, cork, and label. Store in a cool, dark place. Use within 12 months.

Mangoes

Native to the Far East, the Indian subcontinent, and Southeast Asia, the mango was taken by Portuguese explorers to Brazil centuries ago and from there it spread throughout South and Central America, the Caribbean, and Florida, and was then taken to Africa.

There is a huge variety of this tropical fruit—some 2,500 types in all, some ripe when the skin is still green or green flushed with red; others when they become red-gold or pale yellow. Some varieties are fibrous, others less so. Alfonso, Bombay, Haydon, Kent, and Zéphirine are the varieties most often seen.

When you squeeze a mango gently in the palm of your hand, a ripe mango will "give" slightly. The skin, which is inedible, should be smooth and blemish-free. Rich, golden yellow flesh, oozing with juice, is another sign of a ripe mango. Both ripe and underripe mangoes make fine preserves.

PREPARING A MANGO

1 With a sharp knife, cut through the mango lengthwise from each side of the middle to free the seed.

2 Cut the flesh from around the seed, then make evenly spaced crisscross cuts through each side section.

3 Take one side section in both hands and bend it back to separate the cut cubes. Remove these with a knife or spoon, then repeat with the other half.

MANGO CHUTNEY

FILLS 3 1-PINT JARS

This richly fruity chutney is particularly good with a mellow farmhouse cheese and crusty bread, but it is also the classic accompaniment to curries of all types.

2	tart apples, such as Granny Smith
3	large mangoes, peeled and diced
1³/4 cups	golden raisins
3 or 4	chilies, red or green, seeded out, thinly sliced
2 tablespoons	freshly grated gingerroot
	juice and grated zest of 2 limes or lemons
2 cups	soft light brown sugar
2 cups	white wine or cider vinegar
	salt to taste

Peel, core, and dice the apple very small and cook in a nonreactive saucepan with a little water until almost soft. Add the mangoes, the golden raisins, chilies, and gingerroot, as well as the citrus juice and zest, sugar, and vinegar, stirring until the sugar dissolves. Bring to a boil, and simmer until the mixture thickens, 25 to 30 minutes.

Remove the pan from the heat. Skim any foam from the surface. Pot the chutney in hot, sterilized jars, then seal. Process the jars in a boiling-water bath following the method on page 20. Label. Ideally, you should leave the chutney to mature for 2 months before using, to mature the pickle; however, it is also good to eat when freshly made. Use within 12 months.

MANGO KETCHUP

FILLS ABOUT 3 ½-PINT BOTTLES

The ketchup is a very versatile condiment, excellent with broiled or barbecued chicken, lamb, or duck, and is a useful ingredient to paint on meat or fish before broiling it.

1	onion, peeled and finely chopped
3 or 4	ripe mangoes, peeled and diced
1 teaspoon	ground cumin
1/2 teaspoon	mustard seeds
1 teaspoon	freshly grated gingerroot
2	star anise
1	cinnamon stick
1 cup	vinegar—cider, white wine, or distilled
1 cup	soft, light brown sugar

Simmer the onion in the water until almost tender. Add the mango flesh and as much juice as you have been able to retain, as well as the spices, and simmer for 30 minutes or so, stirring frequently. Add the vinegar and sugar and simmer for 15 minutes longer until the mixture thickens.

Remove the pan from the heat. Skim any foam from the surface. When cool, strain, or blend, the ketchup until smooth. Store it in the refrigerator in squeezy bottles with nozzles, which will let you splash and swirl the ketchup on the plate. To keep the ketchup for several months in a cupboard, process it in a boiling-water bath, following the method on page 20. Label. Use within 12 months.

MANGO & YELLOW TOMATO SALSA

FILLS 2 ½-PINT JARS

This bright and lively salsa is an excellent accompaniment to all Tex-Mex dishes, not only meat, but fish, too. It is also delicious with broiled or barbecued prawns, for example.

2	moderately ripe mangoes, peeled and diced
4	yellow tomatoes
1	yellow Scotch Bonnet chili, seeded and sliced
2	shallots, peeled and finely chopped
2 tablespoons	canola oil
2 or 3	scallions, trimmed and finely sliced
2 tablespoons	sugar
3 tablespoons	white wine vinegar
1/2 teaspoon	salt

Heat the oil in a skillet and add the mangoes, tomatoes, chilies, and shallots and cook until soft and cooked tender. Stir the scallions into the mixture, together with the sugar, vinegar, and salt, then simmer gently for about 15 minutes.

Remove the pan from the heat. Skim any foam from the surface. Spoon the salsa into hot, sterilized jars, then seal. Process the jars in a boiling-water bath following the method on page 20. Label. Store in a dark, cool place. Use within 12 months.

COOK'S NOTE: *Scotch Bonnet chilies are among the hottest, so you might want to use less than the whole chili in this recipe. The flavors do become much more concentrated with long keeping.*

MANGO & LIME JAM

FILLS 8 ½-PINT JARS

6	limes, thinly sliced
⅔ cup	water
	juice of 2 limes and 2 lemons
6	large mangoes, diced
4 cups	sugar

Put the sliced limes in a nonreactive saucepan with the water and simmer gently until the fruit is soft. Add lime and lemon juices, and the mango, and simmer for 5 minutes longer. Stir in the sugar and let it dissolve over medium heat, then bring to a boil, and boil until the the setting point is reached.

Remove the pan from the heat. Skim any foam from the surface. With tongs, place the lime slices around the sides where they will be visible, then ladle the jam into hot, sterilized jars, then seal. Process the jars in a boiling-water bath following the method on page 20. Label. Store in a cool, dark place. Use within 12 months.

Melons

When ripe, melons of all varieties should yield to slight pressure at the stem end, and some have an unmistakable melon scent. Take care that melons are well covered if stored in the refrigerator, otherwise they impregnate everything around them with their heady scent. Varieties to look for include cantaloupe, casaba, cranshaw, galia, honeydew, and musk melons, with flesh ranging from pale yellow to dark green.

MELON & MINT PICKLE

FILLS 2 1-PINT JARS

This is a lovely relish for summer meals, and especially good with cold ham or chicken. First you need to make the sweet pickling vinegar (see recipe on page 15).

1 2-pound	melon
1 quart	water
1/3 cup	salt
several sprigs	fresh mint

Halve and quarter the melon, discard the rind and seeds, and cut the flesh into cubes. This is less wasteful than scooping the melon into balls. Put the chunks in a large nonreactive bowl, sprinkle with salt, and pour the water over. Stir a few times to dissolve the salt, then place a plate on top of the fruit to keep it submerged in the brine. Leave for 24 hours, then drain. Put the melon into a nonreactive saucepan with 2 cups sweet vinegar. Simmer for 3 or 4 minutes.

Remove the pan from the heat. Skim the surface for any foam. Pack the melon into hot, sterilized jars, dispersing mint leaves among the melon chunks, fill with hot, sweet vinegar and seal. Process the jars in a boiling-water bath following the method on page 20. Label. Store in a cool, dark place. Use within 12 months.

COOK'S NOTE: *You can also add a few slivers of peeled fresh gingerroot to the brine bath with the melon.*

Nectarines

This smooth-skinned peach is perhaps the most delicious of all stone fruit, at its best in midsummer. The flesh is juicy with a noticeable peach and almond flavor and a good balance of sweetness and acidity. The skin and flesh range from white to yellowy orange to pinkish red. The white-fleshed varieties are particularly fine.

NECTARINE & ALMOND JAM

FILLS 6 ½-PINT JARS

This delicate jam makes a delightful filling for small tartlettes, or can be used to fill a jelly roll.

2	tart apples such as Granny Smith
2/3 cup	water
2 pounds	nectarines, white-fleshed, halved, pitted, and chopped *(there is no need to remove skins, which are soft)*
3 cups	sugar
3/4 cup	slivered almonds

Peel and core the apples, and tie the peel and cores in a cheesecloth bundle or tea filter. Dice the apples very small. Put the apples in a saucepan with the water, and simmer until the fruit is soft. Add the nectarines and continue cooking until these too are just soft and the apple disintegrated.

Using the saucepan lid to hold back the cooked fruit, strain the juices into a preserving pan or other nonreactive pan, and stir in the sugar. Heat gently, stirring, until the sugar dissolves, then boil the syrup for 2 minutes. Add the fruit, stir well, and bring back to a boil. Skim any foam from the surface. Boil until the setting point is reached. Stir in the almonds.

Remove the pan from the heat, and fill the hot, sterilized jars with the jam. Seal. Process the jars in a boiling-water bath following the method on page 20. Label. Store in a cool, dark place. Use within 12 months.

Oranges

Since they grow in abundance in Florida and California, oranges are available all year round. Although there are several varieties, including the large, sweet, almost seedless navel oranges; the smaller blood oranges such as the Moro and Tarocco, with red-flushed skins and deep ruby-colored juice; the Valencia, which is the world's most important orange variety; and the Shamouti, it is the bitter Seville oranges that are best for making marmalade.

Seville oranges have a short winter season and it is worth buying them when you can find them. The season is short because these oranges are traditionally sold unwaxed and they do not, therefore, keep well. However, the fruit can be frozen for making marmalade later in the year.

SEVILLE ORANGE CURD

FILLS 2 ½-PINT JARS

As well as serving this curd as the traditional breakfast and teatime accompaniment, you can also use it to make a number of easy yet luxurious chilled or iced puddings, such as soufflés, parfaits, and ice creams.

3	Seville oranges
2 or 3	sugar lumps
generous ³/4 cup	sugar
1 stick	unsalted butter, cut into pieces
4	large free-range eggs, well beaten and strained

Grate the zest from the oranges, and rub the sugar lumps firmly over the skin to get any last drops of essential fragrant orange oil. Halve and squeeze the oranges. Put the zest, sugar lumps, and juice in the top of a double boiler, or in a stainless steel saucepan, set inside a larger saucepan half filled with simmering water. Add the eggs, butter, and sugar and stir until the sugar dissolves. Continue simmering gently, and stir until the mixture thickens. Doing this in a china bowl set over a saucepan of water and stirring with a wooden spoon can take 45 minutes or so. In a stainless steel saucepan and beating with an electric stick blender the process takes less than 10 minutes.

Remove the pan from the heat. Skim any foam from the surface. Spoon the curd into hot, sterilized jars, cover, and seal immediately. Label, leave to cool completely, refrigerate, and use within 4 weeks, or store in the freezer for 2 to 3 months.

NOTE: *This recipe uses raw eggs.*

COOK'S NOTE: *Extremely rich and rather time-consuming, orange curd, like lemon curd, is something of a luxury. Do not let this put you off making it. Seville oranges are such a rare treat that they deserve being made the most of. I pot my curd in ¹/4-pound jars.*

Fresh curd does not keep long, no more than 4 weeks, and because it uses raw eggs, it must be kept in the coldest part of the refrigerator. However, it does freeze well and will keep for 2 to 3 months.

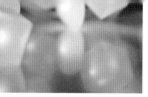

SEVILLE ORANGE MARMALADE

FILLS 6 TO 8 1-PINT JARS

This is the breakfast classic, which appeals to those who like a preserve with a distinct and tangy personality.

3 pounds	Seville oranges
4 pints	water
12 cups	sugar

Rinse the oranges, then put in a large nonreactive saucepan with the water and simmer for an hour or so until soft. Remove the pan from the heat, and leave the fruit to cool.

Halve the oranges, scoop the pulp and seeds into a strainer set over a bowl, and scrape through. Finely slice the orange halves, or process for a few seconds in the food processor. Add the orange peel to the strained mixture and measure.

For every 2 cups of peel and strained pulp, stir in 2 cups cooking liquid, making up the quantity if necessary with water, or lemon juice, or a little of both. Measure it again.

For every 2 cups of this mixture, add 2 cups sugar, and put the mixture in a preserving pan or a large nonreactive saucepan. Heat gently, and when the sugar dissolves, bring to a boil and continue boiling until the setting point is reached; 30 minutes at full boil will do it.

Remove the pan from the heat. Skim any foam from the surface. Leave the marmalade to stand for 15 minutes, then stir to distribute the peel evenly. Fill hot, sterilized jars right to the top, then seal. Process the jars in a boiling-water bath following the method on page 20. Label. Store in a cool, dark place. Use within 12 months.

COOK'S NOTE: *For an extra touch of luxury, you can add a generous splash of whiskey just before potting, for a classic orange and whiskey marmalade.*

After potting marmalade, there is invariably a little left over. Serve it hot over vanilla ice cream, use some to flavor a homemade ice cream, or stir it carefully into a freshly made rice pudding.

ORANGE & APRICOT BUTTER

FILLS 3 1/2-PINT JARS

Not a butter, of course, but a luxurious fruit spread, which you can serve with hot buttered toast, or use as a filling for crêpes or a sauce for desserts and ice cream.

2 cups	dried apricots, coarsely chopped
2 cups	water
2	thin-skinned oranges, thinly sliced and quartered
3 to 3 1/2 cups	sugar
2 tablespoons	lime juice

Soak the apricots in water overnight and, next day, put them and the cut-up orange into a nonreactive saucepan and simmer until the fruit is soft. Rub the mixture through a sieve. Put the pulp, sugar, and lime juice in a nonreactive saucepan and simmer until the sugar dissolves, stirring occasionally. Boil the mixture until thick enough to coat the back of a spoon and stir from time to time to prevent the mixture from sticking.

Remove the pan from the heat and spoon the fruit butter into hot, sterilized jars. Seal and label the jars and when cool refrigerate. It will keep for 2 to 3 months in the refrigerator. For longer keeping, process the jars in a boiling-water bath, following the method on page 20.

Passion Fruit

Originally from Brazil, the passion fruit is now widely cultivated elsewhere in South America, notably Colombia where it is known as *maracuya*, and also in Hawaii and Kenya. By the time it reaches northern stores, it is often shrivelled in appearance.

The true passion fruit *(Passiflora edulis)* in its natural fresh ripe state is a smooth ovoid about 3 inches long with either a reddish purple leathery skin or a pale yellow skin. The fruit is green when unripe; the yellow-skinned fruit has much less flavor.

It is not true that the more wrinkled they are the better; they are just older, and therefore less juicy. The leathery skin encloses a thin reddish pith surrounding a white membranous lining that encloses small, edible crunchy seeds, each one set in a fragrant, intensely flavored, sweet-sour and translucent pulp, dark greenish orange in color.

To obtain the sweet pulp, cut the top off the fruit and spoon out the interior. Both pulp and seeds are edible. If you just want the pulp, rub through a fine strainer with a tablespoon of boiling water, which will help to remove the pulp from the seeds.

PASSION FRUIT VINEGAR

FILLS 2 ½-PINT BOTTLES

As with most tropical fruit, passion fruit has an affinity with shellfish, so you can use this in a dressing for a shellfish salad. Or use it to deglaze the pan after cooking calves' liver or chicken livers.

4	passion fruit
1/4 cup	sugar—*optional*
1 pint	white wine vinegar

Scoop the pulp from the passion fruit and rub it through a strainer with the water. Stir in the sugar if you want to make a sweeter vinegar, then pour the wine vinegar over. Cover and leave overnight for the flavors to develop, then bottle, cork, and label. If you want to, you can strain the vinegar before bottling; however, many cooks like the texture and appearance of the seeds.

PASSION FRUIT CURD

FILLS 4 ¼-PINT JARS

As a filling for cakes and jelly rolls, and as a dessert when combined with meringues and cream or ice cream, passion fruit curd has no equal. It is worth mastering the simple craft of making curd just so that you can make this delectable sweet.

4	smooth passion fruit
1 tablespoon	boiling water
1	lemon
generous ¾ cup	sugar
1 stick	unsalted butter, cut into pieces
4	large free-range eggs, well beaten and strained

Scoop the pulp from the passion fruit as described above, and rub it through a fine strainer with the water into the top of a double boiler, or a stainless steel saucepan set inside a larger saucepan half filled with simmering water. Halve and squeeze the lemon and add the juice to the passion fruit pulp. Add the eggs, butter, and sugar, and stir until the sugar dissolves. Doing this in a china bowl set over a saucepan of water and stirring with a wooden spoon can take 45 minutes or so. Using a stainless steel saucepan and beating with an electric stick blender takes less than 10 minutes.

Remove the pan from the heat. Spoon the curd into hot, sterilized jars, cover, and seal immediately. Label. Leave to cool completely, then refrigerate and use within 4 weeks, or store in the freezer for 2 to 3 months.

NOTE: *This recipe uses uncooked eggs.*

Papaya

Although some varieties grow to an enormous size, the ones I find most often weigh about one pound, and are an elongated pear shape, sometimes slightly angular. The inedible skin turns from green to yellow as it ripens. A traditional test is to look at the stem end of a green papaya; if it has a ring of yellow around it, it will ripen. If not, you will always have an unripe fruit. The seeds at the center of the fruit, although edible, are very peppery.

SWEET CHILI PICKLED PAPAYA

FILLS 5 ½-PINT JARS

This is a fabulous condiment to serve with beef fajitas, and broiled or barbecued steak. First make the sweet vinegar (see recipe page 15).

3 or 4	papayas, weighing about 2 to 3 pounds
⅓ cup	salt
1 quart	water
½ cup	salt
2 or 3	red chilies, thinly sliced
1 pint	sweet vinegar

Halve the papayas, discard the seeds, remove the skins, and cut the flesh into cubes. Put the chunks in a large nonreactive bowl, sprinkle the salt over, and pour in the water. Stir a few times to dissolve the salt, then place a plate on top of the fruit to keep it submerged in the brine and leave for 24 hours.

Drain the papayas, then put them into a nonreactive saucepan with the chilies and 2 cups sweet vinegar. Simmer for 2 minutes, then remove the pan from the heat. Skim any foam off the surface. Pack the pickle into hot, sterilized preserving jars, including the chilies, and top up with vinegar. Seal the jars. Process the jars in a boiling-water bath following the method on page 20. Label. Store in a cool, dark place. Use within 12 months.

Peaches

This sweet, juicy fruit, which originated in China, needs plenty of sun and warmth to ripen it fully, and it is now grown throughout the world. Several varieties can be obtained: yellow-fleshed, pink-fleshed, and perhaps sweetest of all, the small white-fleshed peaches. Some are clingstone peaches, which means the flesh tends to cling to the pit, while others are of the freestone variety.

If you are driving through peach country, in Georgia, in Kentucky, and through Chambersburg, Pennsylvania, famous for its peaches, it is worth buying a bushel basket of these delicious summer fruits. When choosing peaches, look for undamaged and unbruised specimens. The slightest bruise or even firm finger mark will cause the fruit to deteriorate rapidly. The soft, yellow, velvety skin, flushed with red, should not be wrinkled or dry, and the fruit should be firm but not hard.

Peaches make excellent preserves, including chutney, jams, and jellies, and they combine well with oranges to make richly flavored marmalade.

PEACHES IN BRANDY

FILLS 2 QUART JARS

8	white or yellow peaches, skinned and halved, pits discarded, 2 pounds prepared weight
4 cups	sugar
2/3 cup	water
1 teaspoon	pure almond extract
	brandy—*see recipe*

Make a syrup with the sugar and water in a large saucepan, stirring the mixture until it boils. When it is boiling, add the peach halves and almond extract. When the fruit is cooked, remove the pan from the heat and drain it. Leave to cool, then put the fruit into sterilized jars. Half fill the jars with syrup, and then fill to the top with brandy, ensuring there are not any air bubbles. Seal the jars. Shake gently to mix the syrup and brandy. Store in a cool dark place and use within 6 months.

PEACH & ALMOND BUTTER

FILLS 3 ½-PINT JARS

4 cups	chopped peaches
¹/₂ cup	water
3 to 3¹/₂ cups	sugar
2 tablespoons	lemon juice
1 teaspoon	pure almond extract
¹/₂ cup	ground almonds

Put the peaches and water in a saucepan and simmer until the fruit is soft. Rub the mixture through a sieve. Put the pulp, sugar, and lemon juice in a nonreactive saucepan and simmer, stirring, until the sugar dissolves. Then boil the mixture, stirring to prevent sticking, until thick enough to coat the back of a spoon. Stir in the almond extract and ground almonds.

Remove the pan from the heat and spoon the fruit butter into hot, sterilized jars. Seal and label the jars. Refrigerate when cool. It will keep for 3 months there.

PEACH CHUTNEY

FILLS 4 ½-PINT JARS, OR 2 1-PINT JARS

2 cups	sugar
1 pint	cider vinegar
1	tart apple, such as Granny Smith, peeled, cored, and chopped
8	peaches, pitted and each cut in 8 segments
1	onion, peeled and chopped
1 teaspoon *each*	ground cloves, cinnamon, allspice, and cardamom
2 teaspoons	salt

Put the sugar and vinegar in a nonreactive saucepan and bring to a boil, stirring to dissolve the sugar. Add the remaining ingredients, and return to a boil. Reduce the heat and simmer, stirring, until you have a thick, spooning consistency.

Remove the pan from the heat. Skim any foam from the surface. Pot the warm chutney in hot, sterilized jars. Seal. Process the jars in a boiling-water bath using the method on page 20. Label. Store in a cool place. Use within 12 months.

PEACH & ORANGE MARMALADE

FILLS 4 ½-PINT JARS

A fine combination of tangy citrus and mellow peach makes this suitable for both breakfast and teatime.

3	sweet oranges
1	lemon
	water—*see recipe*
6	peaches
	sugar—*see recipe*

Halve the citrus fruit, squeeze the juice into a large measuring jug, and tie any seeds in a piece of cheesecloth, or in a tea filter. Finely shred the citrus peel and put it in a bowl. Add water to the citrus juice to make up to 1 quart, then pour it over the peel and leave overnight to soften.

Next day, put the soaked peel and liquid in a nonreactive saucepan and simmer for about an hour, by which time the peel will be very tender. Halve the peaches, discard the pits, and chop the fruit. Add the fruit to the saucepan and simmer for 10 to 15 minutes longer until the peaches are soft.

Measure the liquid pulp, and for each 2 cups allow 2 cups sugar. Return the pulp to the saucepan and bring to a boil. Stir in the sugar, and when it dissolves, return the mixture to a boil and boil briskly until the setting point is reached.

Remove the pan from the heat. Skim any foam from the surface. Pot the warm marmalade in hot, sterilized jars. Seal. Process the jars in a boiling-water bath following the method on page 20. Label. Store in a cool, dark place. Use within 12 months.

PEACH MELBA JAM

FILLS 6 ½-PINT JARS

Fresh peaches and raspberries are two of the ingredients in the classic dish Pêche Melba, created by the chef Escoffier in honor of the Australian opera singer, Dame Nelly Melba. Spooned over a scoop of vanilla ice cream in a meringue nest, it makes an instant dessert.

1	tart apple, such as Granny Smith
2/3 cup	water
2 pounds	peaches, of any variety, halved, pitted, and chopped
	(there is no need to remove the skins, which are soft)
	juice of 2 lemons
3 cups	sugar
8 ounces	raspberries

Peel and core the apple. Tie the peel and core in a cheesecloth bundle. Dice the apple very small. Put the apples in a nonreactive saucepan with the water, and cook until the fruit is soft Add the peaches and continue cooking until these, too, are soft and the apple disintegrated.

Using the saucepan lid to hold back the fruit, strain the juices into a preserving pan or other nonreactive pan, then add the lemon juice and sugar. Heat gently, stirring until the sugar dissolves, then boil for 2 minutes. Add the cooked apples and peaches, including the raspberries. Stir well and bring back to a boil. Skim any foam from the surface, then boil until the setting point is reached. This will take only a few minutes.

Remove the pan from the heat, and leave to stand for 15 minutes, after which stir to distribute the raspberries evenly. Fill hot, sterilized jars with the jam. Seal. Process the jars in a boiling-water bath following the method on page 20. Label. Store in a cool, dark place. Use within 12 months.

Pears

Although there are said to be more than 5,000 named varieties of pears, almost all descended from the common pear—there are very few varieties on sale at any one time. These include Williams, Anjou, Comice, and Bartlett, although there are also heirloom varieties to be found at local farmers' markets.

SPICED PICKLED PEARS

MAKES 10 SERVINGS

2 cups	red wine vinegar
3 cups	sugar
1	cinnamon stick
12	allspice berries
12	cloves
1/2 teaspoon	blade mace or grated nutmeg
2	bay leaves
10	firm pears

Put all the ingredients, except the pears, in a nonreactive saucepan and heat until the sugar dissolves and then bring to a boil.

Meanwhile, quarter, peel, and core the pears, then place them in a large nonreactive bowl. Pour the boiling liquid over them, cover, and leave overnight. Next day, strain the liquid back into a saucepan, and boil it for 10 to 12 minutes to reduce the volume. Pour the liquid over the fruit and leave to stand for half a day. Boil fruit and syrup together for a minute, then remove the pan from the heat. Skim any foam from the surface.

With a perforated spoon, transfer the pears into hot, sterilized preserving jars. Reboil the syrup, pour it over the pears to within 1/2 inch of the neck of the jar, and process in a boiling-water bath following the method on page 20. Leave to cool, label, and store in a cool, dark place. Keep for at least three weeks before using. Use within 12 months.

PEAR & ORANGE MARMALADE

FILLS ABOUT 8 ½-PINT JARS

For a mellow version of a breakfast marmalade, I have used pears, which round out the flavor and produce a velvet-textured preserve. Use sweet or bitter oranges, according to availability, and remember that a thick-skinned orange produces a more bitter preserve than a thin-skinned orange.

12 pears	Bartlett, Seckel, or Williams, peeled, cored, and sliced
3	oranges, sliced thinly and quartered
5 cups	sugar
2 tablespoons	lime juice

Put all the ingredients in a large nonreactive saucepan. Bring to a boil, stirring until the sugar dissolves, then boil for 20 minutes until the setting point is reached.

Remove the pan from the heat. Skim any foam from the surface. Spoon the marmalade into hot, sterilized jars. Seal. Process in a boiling-water bath following the directions on page 20. Label. Store in a cool place. Use within 12 months.

PEAR & WALNUT JAM

FILLS ABOUT 6 ½-PINT JARS

8	firm pears, peeled, cored, and sliced
1 cup	water
	juice of 1 lemon
1 cup	freshly shelled walnuts
4 cups	sugar

Put the pears and water in a nonreactive saucepan and simmer until the fruit is soft. Stir in the lemon juice, walnuts, and sugar, and simmer gently until the sugar dissolves, then boil briskly until the setting point is reached.

Remove the pan from the heat. Skim any foam from the surface. Pot the jam in hot, sterilized jars, then seal. Process the jars in a boiling-water bath following the method on page 20. Label. Store in a cool, dark place. Use within 12 months.

Persimmons *(also called Kaki, Sharon Fruit)*

The persimmon can be a difficult fruit to buy as there are two varieties which, at a certain stage of their development, look identical—large, slightly elongated orange fruit, with a shiny skin and large calyx.

The true persimmon is exceedingly bitter when underripe, as it is full of tannin. As it ripens it becomes soft and translucent and looks as swollen as a balloon filled with water. The skin puckers when touched, and the tannins will have developed into a mellow sweetness. The time to buy and use persimmons is when they look so overripe as to seem spoiled. Because of this, they are often marked down and one can buy them at a fraction of the usual price.

To use the fruit, slit them open and scoop out the sweet fruit pulp into a large measuring jug, and you are ready to make persimmon jam.

Sharon fruit is a variety of persimmon, grown mainly in California, Israel, and New Zealand, especially bred to be palatable in a conventional state of ripeness. It is sweet but perhaps not quite as luscious as the true persimmon. Its season is from October through November.

PERSIMMON JAM

FILLS 5 ½-PINT JARS

This is an excellent filling for a jelly roll, and equally good to eat when spooned into some plain yogurt.

6	large, very ripe persimmons to make 4 cups persimmon pulp
	juice of 3 lemons
4 cups	sugar

Put the fruit pulp in nonreactive bowl, cover with the lemon juice and sugar, and leave overnight. Stir well, then tip into a nonreactive saucepan. Simmer gently until the sugar dissolves, then boil the mixture until the setting point is reached, 4 to 6 minutes.

Remove the pan from the heat. Skim any foam from the surface. Pot the jam in hot, sterilized jars, then seal. Process the jars in a boiling-water bath following the method on page 20. Label. Store in a cool, dark place. Use within 12 months.

Pineapples

When ripe, this tropical fruit has a mellow smell, a yellow, unblemished skin, and a leaf crown with firm, fleshy leaves. Pull a leaf gently from the middle; when ripe it comes away easily.

PREPARING A PINEAPPLE FOR PRESERVES

1 Holding the pineapple on its side, on a shallow dish to catch all the juices, slice off the leaf crown.

2 Stand the pineapple on its end. With a sharp knife, cut downward to cut away all the skin. Holding it steady, flick out the small, woody eyes with the tip of the knife or a potato peeler.

3 Slice the pineapple crosswise, at 1/2-inch intervals. Lay each slice flat and remove the core with an apple corer, or a knife. Cut each slice into 8 chunks.

PINEAPPLE CHUTNEY

FILLS 5 1/2-PINT JARS

2	tart apples, such as Granny Smith, peeled, cored, and diced
1	large pineapple, peeled and diced
3	green chilies, green, seeded and thinly sliced
2-inch piece	fresh gingerroot, peeled and thinly sliced
	juice and grated zest of 2 lemons
2 cups	sugar
2 cups	cider vinegar

Cook the apples in a little water until almost soft. Add remaining ingredients, then bring to a boil and simmer until the mixture thickens, about 30 minutes.

Remove the pan from the heat. Pot the chutney in hot, sterilized jars. Seal. Process in a boiling-water bath, following the method on page 20. Label. Store in a cool, dark place. Use within 18 months.

PINEAPPLE & GINGER JAM

FILLS 6 ½-PINT JARS

This is a harmonious combination of flavors, in a preserve that has all the traditional uses and some untraditional ones. A scoop of vanilla ice cream with a spoonful of hot Pineapple & Ginger Jam is a palate-stimulating mixture for an impromptu dessert. And consider brushing some of it over duck or pork, before broiling or roasting, especially if you are combining the meat with oriental flavors.

1 piece	fresh gingerroot, about 2 ounces, peeled, thinly sliced, and cut into matchsticks
1	pineapple, prepared
	juice of 2 lemons
4 cups	sugar

Put the gingerroot in a nonreactive saucepan, cover with water, and simmer until almost tender. Add the pineapple chunks and an additional 1 cup water and simmer for about 10 minutes. Add the lemon juice and sugar, stirring until the sugar dissolves. Increase the heat and boil briskly until the setting point is reached.

Remove the pan from the heat. Skim any foam from the surface. Pot the jam in hot, sterilized jars, then seal. Process the jars in a boiling-water bath following the method on page 20. Label. Store in a cool, dark place. Use within 12 months.

PINEAPPLE & ROASTED YELLOW PEPPER SALSA

FILLS 3 ½-PINT JARS

A good source of vitamin C, dietary fiber, and one of the pepsin enzymes that breaks down protein, a pineapple salsa is an excellent condiment to serve with beef fajitas and the steak chimichurra.

1	pineapple, prepared
2	yellow bell peppers
1	mild onion, peeled and chopped
1	red chili, seeded and sliced
1 cup	sugar
1 cup	white wine vinegar
1	garlic clove, peeled and crushed
1 teaspoon	freshly grated gingerroot
	salt and pepper to taste

Cut the pineapple into chunks, half the size as those described on page 102. Roast the peppers over a flame or under a broiler until the skins blister and blacken. Put them in a paper bag, close the end, and leave to steam for a few minutes, which will loosen the skins. Remove the skins by scraping with a knife, then rinse under cold water to remove all traces. Halve the peppers, discard the seeds and stems, and dice the flesh.

Put all the ingredients in a nonreactive saucepan, and simmer until the sugar dissolves. Bring to a boil, and boil for 15 to 20 minutes until the mixture thickens.

Remove the pan from the heat. Skim any foam from the surface. Pot the salsa in hot, sterilized jars and seal. Process in a boiling-water bath following the method on page 20. Label. Store in a cool, dark place. Use within 12 months.

Plums

A widely available stone fruit that comes in several varieties, plums are often available at city farmers' markets in summer and fall, or at roadside farm stands, and it is worth buying plenty as it is so easy to make plum jam. I soon come to regret the spaces in my cupboard in winter if I do not make at least a few jars of plum jam, chutney, and pickles. Most of the fresh plums available in the U.S. are developed from the Japanese plum, and are generally large and round, in skin and flesh colors ranging from pale yellow to deepest red. They include Santa Rosa, Burbank, Friar, Simka, Red Beaut, and Ozark Premier. Some European plums, such as the Victoria and the Italian, as well as the Stanley, an American cultivar of the European plum, are available fresh, but they are largely grown in California for drying as prunes. Occasionally you will find native American plums in the wild, growing on small bushes, especially beach plums near the seashore. These are perfect for preserves.

PLUM JAM WITH ALMONDS

FILLS 5 1/2-PINT JARS

This delicious red jam, lifted with the crunch and flavor of almonds, is at its best for a lazy brunch with toasted English muffins.

3 pounds	plums, halved, pitted, and quartered
1 cup	water
6 cups	sugar
1 1/4 cup	slivered almonds

Put the plums in a nonreactive saucepan, add the water, and simmer until the fruit is tender. Stir in the sugar and when it dissolves, boil briskly until the setting point is reached. Stir in the almonds.

Remove the pan from the heat. Skim any foam from the surface and leave the jam to stand for 15 minutes to distribute the almonds. Pot the warm jam in hot, sterilized jars and seal. Process the jars in a boiling-water bath following the method on page 20. Label. Store in a cool, dark place. Use within 12 months.

PLUM, GINGERROOT & STAR ANISE CHUTNEY

FILLS 8 ½-PINT JARS

Cold roast beef or pork sandwiches are delicious with this mellow, spiced chutney with oriental overtones.

2½ cups	sugar
2 cups	red wine vinegar
4 tablespoons	sherry vinegar
1	large mild onion, peeled and chopped
2	tart apples, such as Granny Smith, peeled, cored and chopped
3 pounds	plums
6	star anise
1 tablespoon	freshly grated gingerroot
½ teaspoon *each*	ground cloves and cinnamon
3 tablespoons	soy sauce

Put the sugar and vinegar in a nonreactive saucepan and stir until the sugar dissolves. Bring to a boil, add the remaining ingredients, bring back to a boil, and reduce the heat, stirring. Simmer until the chutney thickens.

Remove the pan from the heat. Skim any foam from the surface. Pot the chutney in hot, sterilized jars and seal. Process the jars in a boiling-water bath following the method on page 20. Label. Store in a cool, dark place. Use within 12 months.

PLUM ORCHARD PICKLE

FILLS 8 ½-PINT JARS

	juice of 1 lemon
4	firm pears, such as Comice
6	tart apples, such as Granny Smith
2 pounds	plums
½ cup	salt
2½ cups	distilled vinegar
1	cinnamon stick
8	crushed green cardamom pods
heaping ¾ cup	sugar

Squeeze the lemon into a large nonreactive ceramic bowl. Peel, core, and dice the pears and apples, and turn them in the lemon juice. Halve the plums, remove the pits, and cut up the fruit, then add to the bowl. Sprinkle with salt, cover, and refrigerate or keep in a cool place for 24 to 36 hours.

Meanwhile, prepare the vinegar. Since pickling vinegar is already spiced, it does not need long cooking. Put in a nonreactive saucepan with the extra spices and sugar. Heat gently, stirring until the sugar dissolves, then boil for 2 minutes. Remove the pan from the heat and set aside to cool. Drain, rinse, and dry the fruit, then pack it in sterilized jars. Pour the cold, strained vinegar over the fruit, and process in a boiling-water bath, following the method on page 20. Note that this is a cold-pack preserve, therefore time the processing from when the water in the boiling-water bath has reached boiling point. Label the jars and store for at least 2 weeks before using. Use within 12 months.

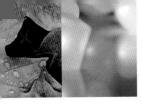

Pomegranates

Although the pomegranate has been of great symbolic significance in many cultures and religions over thousands of years, it has not enjoyed much of a culinary reputation, although some of the uses to which it is put today clearly come from its original home, the Middle East and Central Asia.

When cut in half, the fruit reveals yellow suedelike pith and translucent fleshy cells of juicy red enclosing white seeds. Clusters of cells are separated by a thin yellow membrane that, like the pith and to a lesser degree the seeds, is exceedingly bitter, being full of tannin.

With the juice you can make grenadine, a syrup traditional in France and Italy for flavoring long drinks and ices. Pomegranate syrup is one of the best marinades I know. It has a real depth of distinctive flavor and adds color to the final sauce as might a light red wine. Best of all, it has just the right balance of acidity—for me, preferable to that of lemon or lime.

POMEGRANATE & PINK CHAMPAGNE JELLY

FILLS 4 ½-PINT JARS

This prettily colored jelly makes an excellent gift for family and friends. It is delicious served over ice cream, or served with pancakes or waffles. You can also use it as a glaze for fruit tarts.

2 cups	pomegranate juice
3 cups	sugar
4 to 5 teaspoons	powdered or liquid pectin
1 cup	rosé champagne, or pink sparkling wine
2 teaspoons	lemon juice

Pour the juice into a nonreactive saucepan and stir in the sugar and pectin. Simmer until the sugar has dissolved, then add the champagne and lemon juice. Bring to a boil, then boil until the setting point is reached.

Remove the pan from the heat. Skim any foam from the surface. Pour the jelly into hot, sterilized jars, leaving 1/4-inch headspace. Process the jars following the boiling-water bath method on page 20. Label. Store in a cool, dark place. Use within 12 months.

TO GET THE JUICE FROM A POMEGRANATE

1 Hold the fruit steady and, with a sharp knife, cut a thin slice from the stem end of the fruit, revealing the closely packed, juicy, scarlet seeds inside.

2 Stand the fruit upright and make 5 or 6 knife cuts down through the skin only. Take care not to puncture the seeds as you do this.

3 With your fingers, separate out the 4 or 5 sections, then bend each back and push off the seeds. Remove the bitter pith and membranes and discard.

4 To extract the juice, use the back of a spoon to crush the seeds in a strainer placed over a nonreactive bowl.

Or, simply halve the fruit and extract the juice by gently but firmly pressing each half over a lemon squeezer. It is not a good idea to use an electric or even mechanical means of extracting the juice as this breaks down the seeds and membrane and makes the juice taste too bitter.

POMEGRANATE SYRUP

FILLS 1 ½-PINT BOTTLE

Use the syrup to make pomegranate Margaritas, which are something of a favorite in Mexican restaurants, and have much to recommend them.

I use pomegranate syrup to marinate game, poultry, and lamb. At Christmas I like to prepare nontraditional recipes using traditional ingredients. One year it was pheasant breasts marinated in pomegranate juice and walnut oil, finished off on a charcoal grill. Another year it was sliced, pan-fried turkey breasts, marinated in pomegranate juice, and served with a delicate sauce decorated with pomegranate seeds.

12   pomegranates

Prepare the pomegranates as described above, and extract as much juice as possible: you should have about 1 quart. Pour the juice into a nonreactive saucepan and simmer until it is reduced by three-quarters, resulting in a thick syrup.

Remove the pan from the heat. Skim any foam from the surface. Decant the syrup into a hot, sterilized bottle, then cork and label. If you want to make large quantities for long keeping, process the syrup following the boiling-water bath method on page 20. Use within 12 months.

Quinces

These large, golden-yellow fall fruits are intensely fragrant, with a light fuzzy-gray down on their skins. They belong to the same family as apples and pears and, in shape, can resemble either.

The hard, dry flesh of the quince is a creamy yellow; the seeds and core are very large and coarse. The quince is never eaten raw. Its most important culinary property, apart from fragrance and flavor, is the amount of pectin contained in the seeds, so it makes the most marvellous jams, jellies, and marmalades. Indeed, the word "marmalade" comes from *marmelo*, the Portuguese word for quince.

Quince extract can also be added to fruit less rich in pectin to help give a good set. Quince is perhaps best known for the fruity paste made from the pulp cooked long and slowly with sugar; called *cotignac* or *pâte de coing* in France, and *membrillo* in Spain. The last is often served with soft cheeses or fresh goat's cheese—an excellent combination.

QUINCE JELLY
FILLS 10 ½-PINT JARS

6	large quinces
	water—*see recipe*
	sugar—*see recipe*

Rinse the fruit, but do not peel it, and wipe off the down. Using a sharp, heavy knife, as the fruit is so hard, chop the fruit, including the core. Put the fruit in a nonreactive pan and cover with water, and simmer until the fruit is soft: this can take over an hour. Mash the fruit with a potato masher, then spoon it into a scalded jelly bag suspended over a bowl, and let it drip for several hours, or overnight, without squeezing or forcing. Save the pulp for the following recipe.

Measure the juice and put it in a nonreactive saucepan. For every 2 cups juice add 2 cups sugar and simmer, stirring, until the sugar dissolves. Bring to a boil and boil briskly until the setting point is reached.

Remove the pan from the heat. Spoon the jelly into hot, sterilized jars. Process the jars in a boiling-water bath following the method on page 20. Label. Store in a cool, dark place. Use within 12 months.

QUINCE PASTE

FILLS 2 ½-PINT JARS

Serve this after dinner with a mature hard cheese, with a blue cheese, or a soft goat's cheese, or stir a spoonful into a casserole for a sweet/savory note.

| 1 pound | quince pulp, *see opposite* |
| 2 cups | sugar |

Rub the pulp from jelly-making through a nylon strainer into a saucepan, stir in the sugar, and simmer gently until the sugar dissolves, then continue simmering until the mixture is a translucent garnet color, thick enough to remain separated when you draw a spoon across the bottom of the pan.

Remove the pan from the heat. Spoon the mixture into a heatproof dish, lightly oiled with a neutral oil, such as almond or peanut, then leave the mixture to set. Cut into wedges to serve. Quince paste will keep in the refrigerator for several months.

QUINCE RATAFIA

FILLS 1 PINT BOTTLE

Preserve some of the flavor of quinces by extracting it into a spirit. Use this in cocktails, as an after-dinner digestive, poured over a quince or apple sorbet, or to flambé a hot fruit salad to serve as a dessert.

| 1 or 2 | quinces |
| 2 cups | vodka, gin, or grappa |

Rinse and wipe the quince thoroughly to get rid of the the down on the skin. Cut the fruit into chunks and pack them into a wide-necked decanter or a preserving jar. Cover the fruit with vodka, gin, or grappa. Seal the jar and keep for at least a couple of months for the quince flavor to be absorbed into the spirit.

Strain the ratafia into a measuring jug, then decant into a bottle, seal, and label. Store in a cool, dark place.

Raspberries

A soft, warm crimson red color, with velvety drupelets, the raspberry is a fruit par excellence to enjoy throughout summer. It has a nice tartness that lends itself not only to jams and jellies, but also to a delightful raspberry vinegar.

Contrary to popular belief, fruit vinegars are not a recent invention; raspberry vinegar has been around since at least the days of Queen Victoria. It makes a refreshing drink, diluted with cold sparkling water, as well as being a delicious addition to a vinaigrette.

RASPBERRY JELLY

FILLS 4 ½-PINT JARS

Without seeds, but with a truly glorious color, raspberry jelly is one of the most superior of all preserves. Hot slices of buttered toast or bagels cut in half and toasted are called for!

2 pounds	raspberries, rinsed and drained
	sugar—*see recipe*
	juice of 1 lemon

Put the raspberries in a saucepan with the water and simmer until the fruit is very soft, then crush it with a potato masher. Spoon the puree into a scalded jelly bag suspended over a nonreactive bowl, and let the fruit drip for several hours or overnight without squeezing or forcing.

Measure the liquid and put it in a nonreactive saucepan. For each 2 cups liquid, stir in 2 cups sugar. Add the lemon juice and then simmer, stirring, until the sugar dissolves, then boil briskly, without stirring, until the setting point is reached.

Remove the pan from the heat. Skim any foam from the surface. Pot the jam in hot, sterilized jars. Seal. Process in a boiling-water bath following the method on page 20. Label. Store in a cool, dark place. Use within 12 months.

RASPBERRY JAM

FILLS 6 ½-PINT JARS

Raspberry jam is the classic filling for jam tarts and sponge cakes.

2 pounds	raspberries, rinsed and drained
4 cups	sugar
	juice of 1 lemon

Put the raspberries in a heavy nonreactive pan without any water. Simmer until the juices run, then continue simmering the fruit until some of the liquid has evaporated and the volume reduced by one-quarter to one-third. Stir in the sugar and lemon juice, and when the sugar dissolves, boil the mixture briskly until the setting point is reached.

Remove the pan from the heat. Skim any foam from the surface. Pot the jam in hot, sterilized jars. Seal. Process in a boiling-water bath following the method on page 20. Label. Store in a cool, dark place. Use within 12 months.

RASPBERRY & LAVENDER VINEGAR

FILLS 2 1-PINT BOTTLES

Use this to deglaze the pan after cooking calves' liver or chicken livers for a subtle and unique taste sensation.

2 pounds	raspberries
2 or 3	lavender flower heads
1 quart	white wine vinegar

Put the raspberries and lavender in a large nonreactive bowl, and pour the vinegar over them. Crush the berries with a potato masher, then cover the bowl, and leave to infuse for 1 or 2 days.

Strain the vinegar into a pitcher through a strainer lined with cheesecloth, and then pour into sterilized bottles, cork, and label. Use within 12 months.

Rhubarb

Main-crop rhubarb, available in late spring and summer, is much coarser than early rhubarb, with deep red skin, and a good, if tart, flavor. Winter rhubarb will have been forced and blanched in dark sheds; it is a bright, startling pink.

This rather plain fruit (although strictly speaking a vegetable, we treat it as a fruit) is perfectly partnered by distinctive flavors such as vanilla or gingerroot, and it combines well with other fruit, such as strawberries and pears.

RHUBARB, PEAR & VANILLA JAM

FILLS 6 ½-PINT JARS

2 pounds	rhubarb, rinsed and cut into 1-inch pieces
6	pears, peeled, cored, and sliced
1 packet	fruit pectin
½ cup	water
	juice of 2 lemons
1	vanilla bean
4 cups	sugar

Put the rhubarb, pears, and pectin in a nonreactive saucepan with the water and simmer until the fruit is soft. Stir in the lemon juice, vanilla bean, and sugar and continue simmering until the sugar dissolves. Bring to a boil and then boil until the setting point is reached.

Remove the pan from the heat. Skim any foam from the surface. Remove the vanilla bean and pour the jam into hot, sterilized jars. Rinse and wipe the vanilla bean, and cut it into pieces, sufficient for one per jar. Put a piece into each jar of jam. Seal. Process the jars in a boiling-water bath following the method on page 20. Label. Store in a cool, dark place. Use within 12 months.

RHUBARB & GINGER CHUTNEY

FILLS 6 ½-PINT JARS

This is a classic fruit chutney, to serve with hard cheeses, either in a sandwich or served on the side.

2 pounds	rhubarb, chopped into 1-inch pieces
2	tart apples, such as Granny Smith, peeled, cored, and chopped
thumb-size piece	fresh gingerroot root, peeled, thinly sliced, and cut into matchsticks
2 cups	cider vinegar
2 cups	sugar
½ teaspoon *each*	ground cardamom, cinnamon, and cloves
½ teaspoon	salt

Cook the rhubarb, apples, and gingerroot in half the vinegar until soft, then add the remaining ingredients and simmer until the mixture thickens.

Remove the pan from the heat. Skim any foam from the surface. Pot the chutney in hot, sterilized jars. Seal. Process in a boiling-water bath following the method on page 20. Label. Store in a cool, dark place. Use within 12 months.

RHUBARB & STRAWBERRY JAM

FILLS 6 ½-PINT JARS

2 cups	rhubarb, rinsed and thinly sliced
2 cups	strawberries, rinsed, hulled, and thinly sliced
2 tablespoons	lemon juice
1	packet fruit pectin
5 cups	sugar

In a nonreactive saucepan, cook the fruit in lemon juice and pectin until soft. Add the sugar, stirring until it dissolves, then boil until the setting point is reached.

Remove the pan from the heat. Skim any foam from the surface. Pot the jam in hot, sterilized jars. Seal. Process in a boiling-water bath following the method on page 20. Label the jars. Store in a dark, cool place and use within 12 months.

Strawberries

The large, bright red fruit we know today has developed over the centuries from the tiny wild fragrant fruit that grows throughout many temperate areas.

Of course, the wild or alpine strawberry, *fraise des bois*, is still to be found, growing on wooded banks and enjoyed for its warm, musky flavor. Sweet, white vanilla-flavored strawberries are also occasionally available.

Cultivated strawberries come in many different varieties: small, large, globular, conical, some with a neck, some with a concave top, some with more hairs and seeds than others, some hollow, some dense, and with varying degrees of color.

Look for fruit that is bright, firm, and unblemished with a fresh green calyx (leafy stem) and use it on the same day. If you have to wash the fruit, do so very quickly, and before you remove the calyx, otherwise water will get into the fruit and destroy the delicate flavor.

Apart from jam, strawberry-flavored vinegars and liqueurs can be made by infusing your chosen liquid with plenty of strawberries and keeping it in a dark place for several weeks.

STRAWBERRY CONSERVE

FILLS 2 ½-PINT JARS

With slightly less sugar than jam, the conserve has a softer set and more pronounced fruit flavor. It should be stored in the refrigerator.

1 pound	strawberries, rinsed and hulled
2 cups	sugar

Put the strawberries in a bowl, sprinkle with ½ cup of sugar, and leave in a cool place overnight for the juices to draw out of the fruit. The next day, strain the liquid into a nonreactive saucepan. Add the remaining sugar and stir over low heat, without boiling, for about 10 minutes. Add the strawberries, stir, and simmer for 25 minutes or so or until the setting point has been reached.

Remove the pan from the heat. Skim any foam from the surface. Spoon the jam into hot, sterilized jars. Seal and label. Store in the refrigerator and use this conserve within 2 months.

STRAWBERRY PRESERVE

FILLS 4 ½-PINT JARS

This colorful, elegant, and delectable jam is ideal to serve with warm scones or biscuits topped with whipped cream.

1½ pounds	strawberries, rinsed and hulled
3 cups	sugar
	hot water—*see recipe*
1 tablespoon	fresh or frozen cranberries

Put the strawberries in a bowl, cover with the sugar and 2 tablespoons hot water, and leave overnight.

The next day, strain the syrup into a nonreactive saucepan with 6 tablespoons water and boil for 5 to 10 minutes. Add 1 tablespoon of fresh or thawed frozen cranberries, tied into a damp tea-filter bag, and the strawberries, and boil until the setting point is reached.

Remove the cranberries from the mixture. Remove the pan from the heat. Skim any foam from the surface. Pot the jam in hot, sterilized jars. Seal. Process the jars in a boiling-water bath following the method on page 20. Label. Store in a cool, dark place. Use within 12 months.

COOK'S NOTE: *If you prefer, you can cook the cranberries in the jam, in which case they should be cooked first with the small amount of water, crushed, and then added to the syrup with the strawberries. Spoon the jam into hot, sterilized jars, seal, and label.*

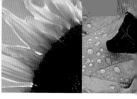

Tamarillo *(also known as Tree Tomato)*

Originally from South America, this fruit is now grown in a number of tropical and subtropical countries, including New Zealand. The fruit is egg-shaped and measures from 2 to 3 inches long. It has a tough but thin and smooth orange-red skin. Tamarillos are ripe when soft to the touch, but the tannin-containing, bitter skins have to be removed before you can eat the fruit. It contains more vitamin C than the average orange. The fruit is very acidic, even when ripe, and makes a well-set jam, salsa, or chutney. It can also be made into toppings by combining it with other fruits; use it in pies, stewed, or dip it into honey and then broil. Tamarillo fruit also makes a fine sweet-and-sour sauce.

TAMARILLO JAM

FILLS 3 ½-PINT JARS

This exotically flavored jam makes a perfect filling for dessert crêpes and is also tasty as a topping for waffles or hotcakes.

8 to 10	tamarillos, stems removed, roughly chopped
	water—*see recipe*
2 cups	sugar

Put the tamarillos in a saucepan with just enough water to barely cover them and cook until very soft. Rub the mixture through a strainer into a saucepan. Stir in the sugar and simmer until the sugar dissolves, then boil until the mixture thickens.

Remove the pan from the heat. Pot the jam in hot, sterilized jars. Seal. Process the jars in a boiling-water bath following the method on page 20. Label. Store in a cool, dark place. Use within 12 months.

VEGETABLES

There is little in the food world quite as varied as vegetables. They come in a huge array of colors, shapes, sizes, and flavors. We seem to be introduced to a new vegetable or a new variety of an existing vegetable almost every week. At the same time old, or heirloom, varieties of vegetables are once again being grown and finding their way into farmers' markets; although they might not always look pretty, their flavor is incomparable.

This chapter does not cover the large-scale canning of vegetables, but the preserving of certain vegetables as pickles, chutneys, salsas, and other relishes that use salt, sugar, and/or vinegar as the means of preserving. More details on this can be found in the chapter on techniques, pages 8 to 25. All of these vegetable preserves will keep in the refrigerator for two or three months, unless a shorter time is specified. If you want to store them for a longer period (in a cool, dry place for a year or more) it is necessary to process the jars in a boiling-water bath, details of which are on page 20. Certain pickles, such as the onions on page 144, which are preserved almost entirely in vinegar, can be stored outside the refrigerator, and without being processed, because vinegar preserves against mold and bacteria.

Tomatoes, squash, eggplants, and bell peppers are really fruits, but we treat them as vegetables, and it is in this chapter that you will find them.

Buying and Preparing Vegetables for Preserving

Whatever vegetables you choose, they should look appetizing and good enough to eat with minimum preparation. Root vegetables should be firm, not limp, with no damp or shiny patches, spade marks, or other surface damage. All root vegetables should be thoroughly washed and scrubbed, in cold water, preferably under the running tap, or otherwise well rinsed before use to get rid of any dirt. Tomatoes, eggplants, and bell peppers should have taut, shiny skins and should be firm and unbruised. Other vegetables, such as fennel, cauliflower, and celery will keep for several days in the refrigerator, at the bottom, but will gradually begin to wilt or become limp and lose their appeal, so it is much better to start preserving soon after you get them home.

Artichokes, Globe Artichokes

The globe artichoke is a member of the thistle family. At its best, the leaves should look fresh and satiny, either pale green or violet, depending on the variety. The head, made up of overlapping club-shaped leaves, should be firm on its stalk, and the leaves should be tightly closed. The small ones, not much larger than 2 inches, are perfect for preserving whole.

To prepare an artichoke, remove and discard the outer leaves and drop each artichoke heart in a nonreactive bowl of water with a splash of lemon juice in it.

ARTICHOKES IN OLIVE OIL WITH LEMON & CORIANDER

FILLS 2 1-PINT JARS

This recipe is perfect when made with small violet artichokes of the poivrade variety.

2 pounds	small violet artichokes
1/2 cup	white wine
6 tablespoons	white wine vinegar
2 teaspoons	salt
1 teaspoon	black peppercorns
1 tablespoon	sugar
1 tablespoon	coriander seeds
1	lemon, quartered and thinly sliced
2	bay leaves
2 cups	extra virgin olive oil

Prepare the artichokes. In a saucepan, bring all the ingredients, except the lemon, artichokes, and olive oil, to the boil.

Remove the saucepan from the heat. Put the lemon and prepared artichokes in a nonreactive bowl, then pour the boiled marinade over them. Leave for 15 minutes, then drain the mix through a strainer set over a nonreactive bowl, leaving the artichokes to cool. When cool, pack the hearts, the lemon, and bay leaves in hot, sterilized jars and fill them with the olive oil. Seal and label the jars, then store in the refrigerator for 2 or 3 weeks before using. Use within 3 months. For longer keeping, process in a boiling-water bath, following the method on page 20.

PICKLED ARTICHOKES & FENNEL SEEDS

FILLS 4 1/2-PINT JARS

Serve these as part of an antipasto or mezze, with olives, sun-dried tomatoes, shallots pickled in balsamic vinegar, and a selection of salamis and cured meats.

2 pounds	baby artichokes
1/2 cup	salt
1 quart	water
2 cups	white wine vinegar
1 cup	white wine
2 tablespoons	fennel seeds
1 tablespoon	white peppercorns
1 1/4 cups	sugar
1/3 cup	olive oil

Prepare the artichokes as instructed on the previous page, then drain the acidulated water and put them in another nonreactive bowl. Mix the salt and water, pour over the artichokes, cover the bowl with a clean dish towel, and leave for 24 hours. Meanwhile, in a nonreactive saucepan, boil the vinegar, wine, fennel seeds, peppercorns, and sugar, then put to one side. Rinse the artichokes and put them in a nonreactive saucepan with the sweet spiced vinegar. Bring to a boil, then boil for 2 to 3 minutes, until just soft, but not cooked through.

Remove the pan from the heat. Skim any foam from the surface. Pack the warm artichokes into hot, sterilized preserving jars, with nonreactive lids. Shake the jars to make sure there are not any air bubbles, topping up with vinegar if necessary. Make sure the artichokes are submerged in the liquid, then float a layer of olive oil on top. Seal and label the jars. Refrigerate and keep for a month before using.

Beets

These ruby-red root vegetables are not my favorite, but they are available most of the year and consequently useful for preserves, especially in the fall and winter months, when fruit is in shorter supply. Golden beets and white beets, as well as a reddish variety with white rings, are also available. Beets are generally pickled after being cooked.

For even cooking, pick vegetables of roughly the same size; make sure the roots are not damaged and the skins are intact. Cut off the leaves about 2 inches above the root. Boil the beets in very lightly salted water until tender, which can take anything from 40 minutes to a couple of hours depending on size. Allow them to cool slightly and rub off the skins. This preparation helps to prevent the beet from bleeding and losing color. The beets are then sliced, packed in preserving jars, and covered with cold spiced vinegar. I rather prefer beet combined with other vegetables and fruit to make a more interesting preserve.

BEET, RED CABBAGE & CRANBERRY CHUTNEY

FILLS 8 ½-PINT JARS

This deep red chutney is excellent with cold cuts of all kinds, and also with vegetable curries. Here, the beets are used uncooked, because chutneys are cooked long enough to soften even the most recalcitrant beet.

8 cups	red cabbage, shredded
4 small to medium	beets, raw, peeled, and shredded or chopped small
1	large onion, peeled and chopped small
1/2 pound	cranberries, fresh or frozen
1 tablespoon	salt
2 teaspoons	mustard seeds
2 teaspoons	peppercorns
2 teaspoons	allspice berries
1 teaspoon	cloves
1 teaspoon	juniper berries
1 teaspoon	cardamom seeds
2 cups	distilled vinegar
1 cup	sugar

Put all the ingredients, except the sugar, in a nonreactive saucepan and simmer until the vegetables are just tender. Stir in the sugar, and when it dissolves, bring the mixture back to a boil then simmer until the mixture thickens.

Remove the pan from the heat. Skim any foam from the surface. Pot the hot chutney into hot, sterilized jars. Process in a boiling-water bath following the method on page 20. Seal and label the jars. Store in a dark, cool place and, if you can keep it for 2 months before opening, you will have a fine mature chutney. Even after a couple of weeks it takes on a distinctive character. Use within 12 months.

SWEET PICKLED BEETS & GINGER
FILLS 2 1-PINT JARS

4 cups	sweet vinegar—*see page 15*
2 pounds	baby beets, washed and scrubbed but not peeled
2-inch piece	gingerroot, peeled, sliced, and cut into thin strips

Simmer the beets in the vinegar in a nonreactive saucepan until tender, up to 2 hours, depending on their age and size.

Remove the pan from the heat, and leave to cool. When cool, remove the beets from the pan and carefully peel them. If they are small, leave them whole, otherwise slice or dice and pack into hot, sterilized jars, distributing the ginger strips evenly. Reboil the vinegar and pour it, through a strainer, over the beets, covering by at least 2 inches. Seal and label the jars. Leave for 2 weeks for the flavor to mature. Store in a cool, dark place. Use within 12 months.

Bell Peppers (see also Chilies)

The bell pepper family includes not only the large, sweet, mild bell peppers now so familiar, but literally hundreds of varieties of hot chilies. Originally we could get only green and red bell peppers, which are a riper version of the green ones, but new strains with vivid and surprising colors have been developed—yellow, orange, white, even black, and lilac. I find yellow and red bell peppers are the most pleasing for preserves, in that their color remains true. Many of the brightly colored bell peppers are simply green bell peppers with a glamorous coat.

Before preserving a bell pepper, I always remove the skin, which is somewhat indigestible. You can peel a pepper with a sharp knife, but by far the best way is to roast or broil it whole until the skin blisters and chars, and can then be rubbed or scraped off. This method gives extra flavor, too. An easy preserve is to slice the cooked bell peppers into long, broad strips, marinate in plenty of olive oil with additional seasoning, put in a preserving jar, and process the jar in a boiling-water bath, following the method on page 20.

BELL PEPPER & RED PLUM JAM

FILLS 6 ½-PINT JARS

This richly colored jam is a revelation, playing on the sweetness of the bell pepper.
Immensely versatile, it can be served with savories or desserts, or on toasted bagels.

8	red bell peppers, peeled, seeded, and chopped
1 tablespoon	salt
1 pound	red-fleshed plums, quartered and stone discarded
1 cup	sweet vinegar—*see page 15*
2 cups	sugar

Salt the peppers overnight in a nonreactive bowl. The next morning, strain and put them in a nonreactive saucepan with the rest of the ingredients. Simmer, stirring until the sugar dissolves, then bring to a boil and boil until the jam thickens.

Remove the pan from the heat. Pot the jam in hot, sterilized jars. Process in a boiling-water bath following the method on page 20. Label and store in a cool dark place. Use within 12 months.

ROASTED BELL PEPPER, GARLIC & ROSEMARY PICKLE

FILLS 4 1/2-PINT JARS

Serve these piquant yellow and red bell peppers with steamed or poached fish for a modern, mighty dish.

3 or 4	large red bell peppers, roasted and peeled
3 or 4	large yellow bell peppers
2	whole heads garlic, cloves peeled
4½ tablespoons	salt
4 sprigs	fresh rosemary, blanched
3 cups	spiced vinegar—*see page 15*
	olive oil *optional, see recipe*

Quarter the bell peppers and discard the seeds and membranes. Cut each piece again lengthwise. Put the pieces of bell pepper and garlic cloves in a nonreactive bowl with the salt, cover, and leave overnight in a cool place. The next day, rinse and drain the peppers and the garlic. Dry on paper towels and pack into hot, sterilized preserving jars. Tuck in the sprigs of rosemary and pour the vinegar over until the vegetables are submerged. You can float a layer of olive oil on top, which also provides a seal. Close the jars and label them. Store in a cool, dry place. Keep for 2 weeks before eating, to let the flavors blend and develop. Use within 12 months.

Chilies

Originating in Mexico, these small, hot members of the Capsicum family were soon introduced into the rest of the tropics by the great explorers, bringing color, heat, and spice to the bland preparations of cassava, yam, corn, and rice, which are still the main staples of these areas.

Chilies deserve respect. To the unwary, they can bring tears and blisters. If you come across a chili you have never seen before, it is safest to assume it is hot until it proves otherwise.

Appearance is some guide to strength: dark green chilies tend to be hotter than pale green ones, and hotter than red, because on ripening to red they sweeten—although "sweet" is a relative term. Also, sharply pointed thin chilies tend to be hotter than short blunt ones. But there are exceptions in all categories and it is possible to get mild and hot chilies from the same plant.

Proceed with caution and take note that some parts of the pod are hotter than others—the tip is milder than the seeds and membranes, so discard both if you are chopping chilies. Wear thin rubber gloves and prepare them under water. Afterward, wash your hands, knives, and chopping board very thoroughly, and, whatever you do, take particular care not to let any part of the chili go near your eyes.

Having said all that, chilies are great fun to use, combined with herbs, fruit or vegetables in a range of exciting preserves! Some of the more common fresh hot chili varieties include: Anaheim, poblano, cayenne, cherry, chili negro, rocotillo, chipotle, habanero, jalapeño, serrano, and Tabasco, but for the purpose of the following recipes, use whatever hot red bell peppers you can find. I prefer red, simply for the color contrast.

In the following recipes, the quantities of chili used will give a preserve with a noticeable chili bite. Reduce the quantity if you prefer a milder preserve.

RED-HOT APPLE & CORIANDER JELLY

FILLS 6 ½-PINT JARS

Serve this with hot or cold meat, poultry, and game dishes and also use it as a glaze on meat or poultry before broiling or roasting. It is especially fabulous with a piece of broiled or barbecued salmon.

2 pounds	tart green apples, such as Granny Smith
2 tablespoons	coriander seeds
2 or 3	red chilies, halved and seeds discarded
	juice of 2 lemons
	sugar—*see recipe*

Wash the apples, then, without peeling or coring them, cut them into chunks and put in a large nonreactive saucepan. Add half the coriander seeds and one of the chilies, sliced. Cover with water, then simmer until the apples are tender and pulpy.

Remove the pan from the heat. Skim any foam from the surface. Strain the pulp through a scalded jelly bag over a nonreactive bowl without squeezing or forcing for 2 hours or overnight.

The next day, measure the liquid and add 2 cups sugar for every 2 cups liquid. Strain the lemon juice into a saucepan, then add the apple extract, sugar, remaining coriander seeds, and the second chili, sliced. Bring the mixture to a boil, then boil for 10 minutes or until the setting point is reached.

Remove the pan from the heat. Skim any foam from the surface. Pour the jelly into hot, sterilized jars, aiming to distribute the coriander seeds and chili pieces equally. Process in a boiling-water bath following the method on page 20. Seal and label the jars. Store in a cool, dry place. Use within 12 months.

RED-HOT PEPPER JELLY

FILLS 6 ½-PINT JARS

This is a very attractive preserve, with lozenges of bell pepper suspended in the pale garnet jelly. It is delicious with cream cheese on a cracker, for an instant snack or hors d'oeuvre, and can also be used as a glaze, brushed over duck breasts or a pork loin before broiling or roasting.

2 pounds	tart green apples, such as Granny Smith
2	red bell peppers, halved, seeds discarded
2 or 3	red chilies, halved, seeds discarded
	juice of 2 lemons
	sugar—*see recipe*

Wash the apples, cut into chunks, without peeling or coring them, and put them in a large nonreactive saucepan, with one of the chilies, sliced. Cover with water, and simmer until the apples are tender and pulpy.

Remove the pan from the heat. Skim any foam from the surface. Pour the apple into a scalded jelly bag placed above a nonreactive bowl and leave to drip, without squeezing or forcing for a couple of hours, or overnight.

Meanwhile, skin the bell peppers as described on page 126 and cut them into diamond shapes.

The next day, measure the liquid, and pour it into a nonreactive saucepan. Add 2 cups sugar for each 2 cups liquid. Add the lemon, the bell peppers, and the chilies. Bring to a boil, then boil until the setting point is reached.

Remove the pan from the heat. Skim any foam from the surface. Pour the jelly into hot, sterilized hot jars, aiming to distribute the pepper and chili pieces equally. Seal. Process in a boiling-water bath following the method on page 20. Store in a cool, dark place. Use within 12 months.

RED-HOT RED CHUTNEY

FILLS 6 ½-PINT JARS

Serve this chutney with curries and other Asian dishes, and as an accompaniment to cold roast meat salads and sandwiches.

2 cups	sugar
4 cups	red wine vinegar
1	large mild onion, peeled and chopped
1	tart apple, such as Granny Smith, peeled, cored and chopped
1½ pounds	red plums
8 ounces	fresh or frozen cranberries
1 pound	tomatoes, quartered and seeded, peeled if you prefer
2 or 3	red chilies, halved, seeds discarded
½ teaspoon *each*	ground coriander and cumin
1 teaspoon	salt

Put the sugar and vinegar in a nonreactive saucepan and bring to a boil, add the rest of the ingredients, bring back to a boil, reduce the heat, then simmer until the chutney thickens.

Remove the pan from the heat. Skim any foam from the surface. Pot the chutney in hot, sterilized jars. Seal. Process in a boiling-water bath following the method on page 20. Label. Store in a cool, dry place. Use within 12 months.

RED-HOT RUBY ORANGE MARMALADE

FILLS 4 1-PINT JARS

This is a new breakfast classic, which appeals to those who like a preserve with an even more distinct and tangy personality! It is also a very fine condiment to accompany roast duck and pork. Or use it, strained, as a glaze before roasting. Look for the ruby-fleshed oranges, which are available during winter months.

8 to 10	ruby or blood oranges
2 or 3	red chilies, halved, seeds discarded, and thinly sliced
2 pints	water
6 cups	granulated sugar

Rinse the oranges, then place them in a large nonreactive saucepan with one of the chilies and the water. Simmer for an hour or so until the fruit is soft. Remove from the heat, and leave the fruit to cool. When cool, halve the oranges, scoop out the pulp and seeds into a strainer set over a nonreactive bowl, then add the chili, and rub through the strainer. Finely slice the orange halves, or process for a few seconds in the food processor. Add the orange peel to the strained mixture and measure the final quantity.

For every 2 cups of peel and strained pulp, stir in 2 cups cooking liquid, making up the quantity if necessary with water, or lemon juice, or a little of both. Measure this mixture again.

For every 2 cups of this mixture, add 3 cups sugar, then put everything in a large nonreactive saucepan, with the remaining chilies. Heat gently, stirring until the sugar dissolves, then bring to a boil and continue cooking until the setting point is reached, about half an hour at full boil.

Leave the marmalade to stand for 15 minutes, then stir to distribute the peel and chili evenly. Fill hot, sterilized jars right to the top. Seal. Process the jars in a boiling-water bath following the method on page 20. Label. Store in a cool, dry place. Use within 12 months.

Cucumber

There are several varieties of cucumber, including the English cucumber, which is a long, slim, straight vegetable with a smooth, dark green, glossy skin. Smaller ridged and even "warty" cucumbers are available, and some are more yellow or white than green. Short cucumbers, also called Kirby cucumbers, are the traditional pickling variety. Select firm, stiff specimens; any that wobble when you pick them up and lightly shake them are old, and will taste bitter and rubbery. A good cucumber will be moist, juicy, and crisp inside, with a good proportion of flesh to seed.

The cucumber is 96 percent water, so the trick in using them for preserves is to get rid as much of that water as possible, which you do by salting them. It is also a good idea to remove the watery core and seeds.

CUCUMBER & DILL PICKLES

FILLS 4 ½-PINT JARS

This delicious sweet pickle is simple to make, and is better than most pickles you can buy.

5 large	English cucumbers, quartered and seed core removed
1/2 cup	salt
2 tablespoons	dill seeds
	fresh dill *(if available)* or 2 to 3 tablespoons dried dill weed
3 cups	cider vinegar
2 cups	sugar

Cut the cucumbers into slices to fit the jars you are using. Put the pieces in a nonreactive bowl, then mix in the salt. Cover the bowl with a clean dish cloth, and leave for 24 hours.

Meanwhile, boil the vinegar, sugar, and dill seeds, then remove the pan from the heat and put to one side. Rinse and dry the cucumber pieces, making sure you have washed off most of the salt, then pack them into two sterilized jars while they are still warm. Distribute fronds of fresh dill or sprinkle the dill weed among the cucumber pieces, then pour the vinegar and dill seeds over the cucumber. Shake the jars to make sure there are not any air bubbles; top up with vinegar if necessary. Make sure the cucumber is submerged in the liquid, then seal and label the jars. Try to keep for a month before using. Use within 12 months.

ORIENTAL PICKLED CUCUMBER & CARROT

FILLS 4 ½-PINT JARS

This is a marvellous accompaniment to cold noodle salads, with chicken, shrimp, or vegetables.

3	large English cucumbers, halved, cores and seeds removed
4	medium carrots, scrubbed and peeled
thumb-size piece	fresh gingerroot, peeled and thinly sliced
6 tablespoons	salt
2 cups	distilled white vinegar
1 or 2	lemongrass stems
	grated zest of a lime
1 to 2 tablespoons	lime juice
1 tablespoon	Szechuan peppercorns
2	star anise
1	cinnamon stick
1½ cups	sugar
1 tablespoon	fermented black beans
3 tablespoons	toasted sesame oil

Cut the cucumber into slices about ½ inch thick. Slice the carrots into pieces about half the thickness of the cucumber. Cut the gingerroot into strips. Put these ingredients into a nonreactive bowl with the salt, loosely cover, and leave in a cool place for 24 hours.

Meanwhile, put the vinegar, lemongrass, lime zest and juice, peppercorns, star anise, cinnamon, and sugar in a saucepan, and then put the beans in a nonreactive bowl. Bring the ingredients in the pan to a boil, then simmer until the sugar dissolves. Pour this mixture over the beans, then leave in the bowl overnight.

The next day, rinse the vegetables, then dry on paper towels. When they are dry, pack them into the preserving jar and fill with the infused vinegar, including the spices and black beans. Shake the jar to make sure there are no air pockets, and top up with vinegar if necessary. Make sure the vegetables are submerged, and float the sesame oil on top before sealing the jar. Label. Keep in the refrigerator. Use within 2 to 3 months.

Fennel, Bulb Fennel *(also called Florence Fennel)*

The sweet, anise flavor of fennel is like that of no other vegetable I know. Fennel resembles a squat head of celery, white with overlapping ridged leaves. Sometimes the fine green frondlike leaves are left on, sometimes not. Look for fennel bulbs that are well rounded. Flat-bellied ones are immature. Specimens should not show any bruising or broken leaves, and they should look dry, but not dried out.

Use fennel that is fresh, although it will keep in the salad drawer of the refrigerator for a few days. Cut surfaces will brown when exposed to the air, so when you slice it, drop the pieces into acidulated water immediately.

FENNEL & CHILI JELLY

FILLS 4 ½-PINT JARS

Serve this as an accompaniment to roast pork or roast duck, and with sandwiches, wraps, or fajitas made with either of these meats. Or try a spoonful of the jelly with fresh goat's or other soft cheese.

4	tart green apples, such as Granny Smith
2	red chilies, halved, seeds discarded, sliced
2	large fennel bulbs
	juice of 2 lemons
	sugar—*see recipe*

Wash the apples, cut into chunks, without peeling or coring them, and put in a large nonreactive saucepan, with one of the chilies, and the outer leaves and fronds of fennel, chopping the outer leaves. Cover with water, and simmer until the apples are tender and pulpy.

Remove the pan from the heat. Skim any foam from the surface. Strain the pulp through a scalded jelly bag without squeezing or forcing; otherwise, the jelly will be cloudy.

Meanwhile, halve the fennel, then thinly slice so that each slice has several layers of leaves, just attached at the base. Then measure the strained apple liquid, and add 2 cups sugar for every 2 cups liquid. Strain the lemon juice into a nonreactive

saucepan, then add the apple extract, sugar, sliced fennel, and chili. Bring everything to a boil, and boil for 10 minutes or until the setting point is reached.

Remove the pan from the heat. Skim any foam from the surface. Pour the jelly into hot, sterilized hot jars, aiming to distribute the fennel and chili pieces equally. Seal. Process in a boiling-water bath following the method on page 20. Label. Store in a cool, dry place. Use within 12 months.

SWEET FENNEL & ONION MARMALADE

FILLS 4 ½-PINT JARS

This is delicious served as part of a mezze or hors d'oeuvre with, for example, sardines, hard-boiled eggs, and olives.

4	large mild onions, peeled and thinly sliced
6 tablespoons	extra virgin olive oil
3	large round fennel bulbs, sliced
6 tablespoons	white wine
1 teaspoon	ground cumin
1 teaspoon	ground coriander
1 teaspoon	salt
1 teaspoon	freshly ground black pepper
3 tablespoons	sultanas or raisins
3 tablespoons	toasted pine nuts or flaked almonds
1 cup	white wine vinegar
1½ cups	sugar

Fry the onion in oil for 10 to 15 minutes over low heat, then add the fennel, wine, cumin, and coriander. Continue simmering for 15 to 20 minutes, stirring from time to time to prevent sticking. Add the salt and pepper, then stir in the fruit, nuts, and wine vinegar. Bring to a boil, then boil for 5 minutes, until the vegetables are soft. Add the sugar, stirring until it dissolves. Simmer until the mixture has a soft consistency, and the vinegar and cooking juices have been absorbed.

Remove the pan from the heat and pot the marmalade in hot, sterilized jars. Seal. Process in a boiling-water bath following the method on page 20. Label. Store in a cool, dry place. Use within 12 months.

SWEET FENNEL & ORANGE PICKLE

FILLS 4 ½-PINT JARS

3 ½ cups	sweet vinegar—*see page 15*
½ cup	fresh orange juice
2 pounds	miniature fennel, left whole
or	
2 or 3	large Florence fennel bulbs, rinsed and cut into wedges
	thinly pared zest of 2 oranges

Simmer the fennel in the sweet vinegar and orange juice in a nonreactive saucepan until tender, 30 to 45 minutes, depending on age and size.

Remove the pan from the heat, and leave the contents to cool. When cool, remove the fennel from the pan and pack the vegetable into hot, sterilized jars, distributing the orange zest so it is visible. Reboil the vinegar and pour it, through a small strainer, over the fennel, covering by two inches. Seal and label the jars and leave for a week or two for the flavor to mature. Use within 12 months.

Garlic

This is a member of the large Allium genus to which chives, onions, shallots, and leeks also belong. There are white-skinned, pink-skinned, and purple-skinned varieties—the purple- and pink-skinned varieties are generally considered to be superior.

Garlic is available all year round since, like onions, it can be dried and stored. However, new season's garlic is a wonderful treat to look forward to in late spring. Old garlic might be beginning to shoot, a green tip emerging at the pointed end. The garlic can still be used, but cut the clove in half and completely remove the small green shoot, which has a strong, bitter taste.

MOJO ROJO (RED SAUCE)

FILLS 3 ½-PINT JARS

This is a versatile sauce you can add to casseroles and soups for a hint of piquancy.

8 to 10	mild red chilies, stem and seeds removed
	water—*see recipe*
2	heads garlic, cloves peeled, blanched for 2 minutes in boiling water, and drained
1 tablespoon	cumin seed, lightly toasted
2 tablespoons	coarse sea salt
6 tablespoons	sweet pimento/paprika
1 cup	aged red wine vinegar
2 cups	olive oil
½ cup	toasted, ground almonds

Place the red chilies in a nonreactive saucepan with enough water to cover generously. Bring to a boil, then remove the pan from the heat and leave the chilies to soften for a few hours. When soft, drain the chilies on paper towels and pat dry.

The sauce can then be made either in a mortar, pounding the solid ingredients first, or in a food processor, chopping the solid ingredients first. Whichever method you use, gradually add the oil and vinegar to make an emulsion. Leave in a cool place for 2 days for the flavors to develop, then pot in hot, sterilized jars. Seal. Process in a boiling-water bath following the method on page 20. Label. Store in a cool, dry place. Use within 24 months.

MOJO VERDE (GREEN SAUCE)

FILLS 2 ½-PINT JARS

Mojo verde is the perfect accompaniment to broiled or fried fish, such as salmon, sea bass, grouper, or tuna. Also try it as an accompaniment to broiled or breaded and deep-fried goat's cheese served on a heap of salad leaves.

2 teaspoons	sea salt
2 heads	garlic, with cloves peeled and chopped
1 teaspoon	cumin seeds, lightly toasted
1	green bell pepper, seeds and stem removed
	(use a green chili if you want more piquancy)
bunch	fresh coriander
smaller bunch	fresh parsley
about ⅔ cup	olive oil
about ⅔ cup	red wine vinegar
	water for thinning *(optional)*

Using a food processor, or pestle and mortar, make a paste with the salt, garlic, and cumin, then add the bell pepper, and the leaves only of the coriander and parsley. When this is well mixed, add the oil and vinegar. If the mixture is too thick, thin it down with water.

Leave in a cool place for 2 days for the flavors to develop, then pot in clean, sterilized jars. This sauce keeps well when refrigerated in an airtight container. If you are planning to store the sauce at room temperature, process it in a boiling-water bath following the method on page 20. Seal and label. Store in a cool, dry place. Use within 12 months.

Okra *(also called Ladies' Fingers)*

Okra is the name for an edible seedpod belonging to the hibiscus and mallow family. A Southern specialty, the small, tapering, five-sided pods are about 2 to 4 inches in length. Choose firm, small, bright green ones that still have a fresh-looking bloom, snap cleanly, and do not bend. Avoid any that are browning at the edges and tip.

To prepare for preserving whole, wash and dry them, and carefully pare off the stem without breaking the seedpod. Inside are tiny edible seeds and a sticky juice. In the following recipe, the juice combines with the spices, mustard, vinegar, and sugar to bathe the vegetables in piquant sauce.

PICKLED OKRA

FILLS 5 1-PINT JARS

2 pounds	fresh, small okra
4 cups	sweet vinegar—*see page 15*
10	garlic cloves, peeled
5	small whole red chilies

Soak the okra in water for an hour, then drain it. In a nonreactive saucepan, bring the vinegar to a boil. Pack the okra alternately top to tail in hot, sterilized jars, and tuck a couple of garlic cloves and a chili round the edge of each jar.

Remove the saucepan from the heat. Cover the okra with the boiling vinegar, then seal the jars. Process in a boiling-water bath following the method on page 20. Label the jars and store in a cool, dark place for at least 3 weeks before eating. Use within 12 months.

OKRA, EGGPLANT, TOMATO & CORN RELISH

FILLS 4 1-PINT JARS

This mustardy, sweet-savory relish will accompany hamburgers, broiled dishes, and barbecues to perfection.

1 pound	fresh okra, prepared and sliced
1	eggplant, peeled and diced into small pieces
1 pound	tomatoes, halved and seeded
2 heads	sweet corn kernels, roughly chopped
4	garlic cloves, peeled, diced in 2 or 3 pieces
1	onion, peeled, thinly sliced
1 cup	salt
6 cups	water
4 cups	plain vinegar
4 cups	spiced vinegar—*see page 15*
3 tablespoons	plain flour
3 tablespoons	dried mustard
1 tablespoon	mustard seeds
1 teaspoon	ground turmeric
1³/4 cups	sugar

Put all the vegetables in a nonreactive bowl and cover with salt and water. Stir well, then cover and leave for 24 hours.

The next day, drain well, put the vegetables back in the bowl, and cover with plain vinegar for 12 hours. In a small nonreactive bowl, make a paste with a little of the spiced vinegar, flour, mustard, mustard seeds, turmeric, and sugar. Put the remainder of the spiced vinegar in a nonreactive pan, stir in the paste, bring to a boil, then add the drained vegetables. Simmer for 20 minutes.

Remove the pan from the heat. Skim any foam from the surface. Pack the relish into hot, sterilized jars, and seal. Label. The double dose of vinegar ensures that this relish will keep well. Store in a cool, dry place. Use within 12 months.

Onions

This is the vegetable that cooks never allow themselves to run out of.

With the exception of scallions, most of the onions on sale have been allowed to dry out slightly, hence their crisp, papery skin. Choose firm, dry specimens with thin, light skins, which might or might not be peeling off. Avoid any that are obviously damaged, are soft, or show signs of dampness, and any that are beginning to sprout green shoots.

For pickling, use any small-bulb onions, but the brown-skinned, white-fleshed varieties are the most popular for this. They are sometimes called pearl onions or button onions.

PICKLED ONIONS

FILLS 5 ½-PINT JARS

I love to pickle onions with red wine, sugar, and herbs such as thyme or marjoram, then serve them with cold roast beef. First, they need brining and steeping in pickling vinegar.

2 pounds	pickling onions, peeled
1 cup	salt
8 cups	water
4 cups	distilled vinegar
2 cups	red wine vinegar
1 cup	sugar
1 sprig *each*	thyme, marjoram, and oregano

Put the onions in a bowl with half the salt and half the water, then cover and leave for 2 days. Drain them and repeat the process with the rest of the salt and water, cover and leave for a further 2 days. Drain them and cover with the plain vinegar, and leave for 2 days longer.

Meanwhile, put the red wine vinegar and sugar in a nonreactive saucepan, bring to a boil, then put to one side. Drain the steeped onions and pack them into jars with nonreactive lids. Tuck in the herbs, and pour the sweet vinegar over. Shake the jars to make sure there are not any air bubbles. Top up with more vinegar if necessary. Seal. Label, then leave for a month to mature. Use within 12 months.

SAGE & ONION JELLY

FILLS 5 ½-PINT JARS

Here is a new twist to pork's favorite accompanying flavors. Serve the jelly on the side with broiled or roasted pork, or use it to glaze a roast duck or a pork loin roast.

2 or 3	large onions, peeled and roughly chopped
1	tart apple, such as Granny Smith, roughly chopped *(do not peel or core)*
2 cups	water
½ cup	white wine vinegar
	sugar—*see recipe*
1 packet	fruit pectin
1 to 2 tablespoons	fresh sage leaves, chopped

Put the onions and apple in a nonreactive saucepan with the water. Simmer until both are soft. Mash with a potato masher, then spoon into a scalded jelly bag suspended over a bowl, without squeezing or forcing, for at least two hours, or overnight if possible.

The next day, measure the liquid into a nonreactive saucepan, and for every 2 cups, add 2 cups sugar, together with the vinegar, pectin, and sage. Simmer over a low heat until the sugar dissolves, then boil until the setting point is reached.

Remove the pan from the heat. Spoon the jelly into hot, sterilized jars and seal. Process in a boiling-water bath following the method on page 20. When cool, label and store the jars in a cool, dark place. Use within 12 months.

Peanuts

Although the peanut (also called groundnut, monkey nut) is not a nut but a member of the legume family that grows underground, the peanut's culinary position lies closer to that of the nut than the bean.

It is a highly nutritious product from which a high-quality oil, eminently suitable for cooking, is derived. But for the home cook, it is worth buying a batch of peanuts every now and then to make your own peanut butter. It is so good and easy to make that you will probably never buy another jar again. And your friends will love it.

PEANUT BUTTER

FILLS 4 ¼-PINT JARS OR 1 PINT CONTAINER

As well as using to make the classic peanut butter and jelly sandwich, peanut butter is also good to use in Southeast Asian dishes, such as a sauce for satays, and also in home baking—peanut butter cookies are delicious.

2 pounds	roasted peanuts in the shell
	salt—*optional*
	peanut oil—*see recipe*

Buy the freshest toasted peanuts you can and shell them. You will find that having been toasted first, the nuts will readily shed their papery skin. This should be discarded, along with the shell. Put all the nuts in a food processor, then pulse the motor first to crush them, then keep the motor switched on until the nuts begin to oil and become smooth. If the nuts are fresh, they will contain all the oil needed to make a smooth butter. If not, you can add a drop of peanut oil. You might also want to add a pinch of salt, but do not add sugar, as there really is no need, despite its being on the contents list on many jars of peanuts.

Store the peanut butter in an airtight container in the refrigerator, and use within 2 months.

Pepper — *see Bell Pepper*

Pumpkins

Perhaps the best known of all the fall and winter squashes, these hard-skinned, brilliant orange vegetables can grow to an enormous size; one specimen is recorded as weighing in at 400 pounds. Usually, they are more manageable: "pie pumpkins" can be found at around 6 pounds, and the variety Jack-Be-Little is tiny, up to 2 pounds in weight. Even so, many pumpkins are larger than the average household might want (unless a pumpkin lantern is required) and so they are often sold by the piece. If buying it by the piece, check that the orange flesh is firm, not fibrous.

PUMPKIN JAM WITH RUM, HONEY, & VANILLA

FILLS 8 1/2-PINT JARS

This beautiful golden preserve, with its tropical hints of rum and vanilla, is exquisite spooned over vanilla or rum and raisin ice cream.

3 pounds	pumpkin, rind and seeds discarded, cut into pieces
4 cups	water
2	vanilla pods
	juice of 2 lemons
1/2 cup	clear honey
4 cups	sugar
1/2 cup	rum

Slice the pumpkin pieces very thin. Put them in a nonreactive saucepan with the water, vanilla pods, and lemon juice. Simmer for 10 minutes, until the pumpkin is just soft, but not collapsing—you want to try to retain the nice, thin slices—then add the honey and sugar. Stir until the sugar dissolves, then bring to a boil and boil for 10 minutes. Add the rum, then boil until the setting point is reached.

Remove the pan from the heat. Skim any foam from the surface. Take out the vanilla pods, and when cool enough to handle halve them, split each half in two. Scrape the seeds back into the jam and stir to distribute them. Put a piece of vanilla pod in each hot, sterilized jar before you spoon in the jam. Process the jars in a boiling-water bath following the method on page 20. Seal and label the jars. Use within 12 months.

PUMPKIN & SPICE CHUTNEY

FILLS 4 1-PINT JARS

Here I use some of the sweet spices more usually associated with pumpkin pie. They make a surprisingly good chutney, sweet and sour, with delicate spicing and a little kick from the peppercorns and ginger. I love it with cold turkey during the holiday season.

3 pounds	pumpkin, peeled, seeded, and diced into 1-inch chunks
4	tart apples, such as Granny Smith, peeled, cored, and sliced
thumb-size piece	fresh gingerroot, peeled, sliced, and cut into strips
1 tablespoon	pink peppercorns
1 tablespoon	black peppercorns
1 tablespoon	cardamom seeds
1 tablespoon	coarsely grated nutmeg
8	cloves
2	cinnamon sticks
4 cups	white wine vinegar or distilled vinegar
2 cups	soft brown sugar
1 tablespoon	salt

Put the pumpkin, apples, ginger, spices, and half the vinegar in a nonreactive saucepan, stir, and bring to a boil. Reduce the heat and simmer for 15 minutes, then add the remaining vinegar and simmer for 15 minutes more before adding the sugar and salt. Stir, bring back to a boil, and simmer for about an hour until the chutney has cooked to a thick, jam-like consistency, with most of the cooking liquid evaporated.

Remove the pan from the heat. Pot the chutney in hot, sterilized jars. Process in a boiling-water bath following the method on page 20. Then seal and label. Keep for 3 to 4 weeks for the flavors to develop before using the chutney, although it is very good to eat within a few days! Use within 12 months.

Tomatillos

A member of the *Physallis* family, and resembling pale green tomatoes with a papery husk, tomatillos are also called husk tomatoes. Originating in Mexico, they are much used there in salsas and other savory dishes. Since their introduction into the U. S. their use has extended to a wider range of relishes and preserves, including jams and ketchups. When ripe, the fruit turns a very pale yellow and bursts out of its light brown husk. I prefer to use its distinctive, slightly sharp flavor combined with onions, sugar, chilies, lime juice, and salt in a simple salsa.

TOMATILLO COOKED SALSA

FILLS 4 ½-PINT JARS

This is perfect with all Tex-Mex and southwestern dishes.

2 pounds	tomatillos, husks removed, roughly chopped
1	tart apple, such as Granny Smith, peeled and cored, roughly chopped
2	large onions, peeled and chopped
2 or 3	green chilies, sliced, seeds and membranes removed
2 or 3	cloves garlic, peeled and sliced
1 cup	sugar
	juice of 4 limes
1/2 cup	white wine
	white wine vinegar—*see recipe*
8 to 10	sprigs fresh coriander

Put the tomatillos and apples in nonreactive saucepan with the onion, chilies, garlic, and sugar. Make up the lime juice, white wine, and wine vinegar to 2 cups, then add to the pan. Stir well, bring to a boil, and simmer for an hour until the mixture has thickened. Add the coriander leaves, mix well, then remove the pan from the heat. Skim any foam from the surface. Pot the salsa in hot, sterilized jars with nonreactive lids. Seal. Process in a boiling-water bath following the method on page 20. Label. Store in a cool, dark place. Use within 12 months.

Tomatoes

Increasingly farmers' markets and pick-your-own farms sell heirloom tomato varieties, of which there are something in the order of 500. Names range from Abe Lincoln and Amish Gold to Wolford's Wonder and Yellow Ruffled via Grandpa's Minnesota, Hawaiian Currant, Kentucky Beefsteak, and Missouri Pink Love Apple. These prettily colored fruit, often exotically striped or multicolored, are perhaps best enjoyed *au naturel*, as they attract a premium price.

Instead, commercial hybrids make perfectly acceptable preserves. Look for firm but ripe fruit. Red tomatoes should look red, not orange. Varieties include Beefmaster, Brandywine, Carmello, Celebrity, Delicious, Dona, Early Girl, Enchantment, Lemon Boy, Pink Girl, Red Cherry, Small Fry, Sweetie, and Tiny Tim. Names will often be a good guide to either size or color. Lemon Boy, for example, is a delicately flavored yellow tomato.

Generally I find that plum tomatoes are firmer and less juicy, which makes them ideal for drying and for preserving.

TO SKIN, OR NOT TO SKIN TOMATOES?

If you are using the tomatoes uncooked or very briefly cooked, or if you are straining them, there is no need to skin them. If you are cooking the tomatoes slowly, as when making chutney, I recommend skinning them, otherwise the skin will gradually loosen, detach, and roll into a tight little quill, not very digestible or pleasant to eat.

TO SKIN TOMATOES

Remove the green calyx and a small piece of the tougher core. Cut a cross in the other end of each tomato. Lower the tomatoes into a bowl of water which has just been boiled and leave them there for about 30 seconds. Drain the tomatoes and peel back the skin. It should come away very easily.

Dried tomatoes

Dried tomatoes are a useful form of preserved tomato and store well. They have a dense texture and a concentrated flavor which makes them useful for adding to slow-cooking casseroles, minestrone soup, and pasta sauces.

TO MAKE SUN-DRIED TOMATOES

A very simple pasta sauce can be made by cutting sun-dried tomatoes into thin strips and stirring them with olive oil and crushed garlic into a bowl of freshly cooked pasta.

- Plum or other intensely flavored tomatoes, halved
- Coarse sea salt
- at least 6 consecutive hot, sunny days

I first learned how to prepare these on a Mediterranean island, Gozo, in the early 80s, before they had become a fashionable ingredient but were simply what the islanders did with their abundant tomato crops. We spread the halved tomatoes in shallow, wooden fruit trays, sprinkled them with sea salt, and left them in the sun, covered with netting to protect them from insects, all day. At sundown, we brought them indoors, otherwise the dew would have undone all the sun's drying. As we put them out in the sun again next morning, we pressed each tomato lightly, with two fingers, bringing more moisture to the surface, which would evaporate by the end of the day. In high summer it takes about 6 days for the tomatoes to become dry enough to pack, lightly oiled, in jars, which you then seal and label.

You can use a similar method for oven drying, but in this case, leave them in the oven on low heat until dry, about 6 to 8 hours. A fan oven is particularly suitable for this task.

ROASTED TOMATO, FENNEL, & RED PEPPER PICKLE

FILLS 4 ½-PINT JARS

1 large	fennel bulb, weighing about 1 pound
2	sweet red bell peppers, cut into quarters, seeds discarded
4	large tomatoes
½ cup	salt
1¼ pint	spiced vinegar—*see page 15*
1 teaspoon *each*	cumin and coriander seeds
8	crushed cardamom pods
¾ cup	sugar

Cut the large fennel bulb into 8 wedges, depending on size and shape, and brush with oil. Then place all the vegetables in a broiling or roasting dish, and broil or roast the vegetables for about 10 to 15 minutes. The fennel will still be relatively firm. Skin the bell peppers and tomatoes when cool enough to do so, then put the vegetables in a nonreactive bowl. Sprinkle the salt over, cover, and refrigerate, or keep in a cool place for 24 to 36 hours.

Meanwhile, prepare the vinegar. Since it is already spiced, it does not need to cook for long. Put in a nonreactive saucepan with the spices and sugar. Heat until the sugar dissolves, then bring to a boil and boil for 2 minutes. Leave to cool. Rinse the vegetables thoroughly. Drain and dry them, then pack in hot, sterilized preserving jars. Pour the cold, strained vinegar over the vegetables, then seal and label. Store in a cool, dark place for a couple of weeks before using to let the flavors develop and mature. Use within 12 months.

SPICED TOMATO & GARLIC CHUTNEY
FILL 3 ½-PINT JARS

2 pounds	ripe tomatoes, skinned, roughly chopped
1	large mild white onion, peeled and diced
	cloves of a whole head of garlic, peeled and sliced
1	fresh red chili, halved, seeds discarded, thinly sliced
6	cardamom pods, cracked
6	cloves
1 cup	sugar
1 cup	red or white wine vinegar
1 teaspoon	salt

Put all the ingredients in a large, nonreactive saucepan and bring to a boil. Simmer for about an hour until the mixture thickens to a pulpy consistency, stirring from time to time to stop the mixture sticking.

Remove the pan from the heat and leave the mixture to cool a little. Stir, then spoon into hot, sterilized jars. Seal. Process in a boiling-water bath following the method on page 20. Label. Store in a cool, dry place. Use within 12 months.

TOMATO, ORANGE & GINGER JAM
FILLS 8 ½-PINT JARS

4 pounds	firm, ripe tomatoes, peeled, quartered and seeded
2	oranges, halved, seeded, and thinly sliced
4	thin slices gingerroot, peeled and cut into shreds
	juice of 2 lemons
5 cups	sugar

Combine all the ingredients in a nonreactive saucepan and cook over low heat until the sugar dissolves, then boil until the jam thickens and looks translucent, about 40 minutes. Stir to prevent sticking.

Remove the pan from the heat. Spoon the jam into hot, sterilized jars. Seal. Process in a boiling-water bath, following the method on page 20. Label and store in a cool, dark place. Use within 12 months.

TOMATO SALSA

FILLS 4 1-PINT JARS

This is the classic salsa found in Mexican restaurants, piquant and full of ripe flavors. It is only worth making in high summer, when tomatoes are at their peak of perfection.

4 cups	peeled, cored, and chopped tomatoes
2 cups	seeded, chopped red or green bell peppers
6	jalapeño peppers, seeded and chopped
1	onion, peeled and finely chopped
4	cloves garlic, finely chopped
2 cups	red wine
1 teaspoon	ground cumin
1 tablespoon	oregano leaves
1 tablespoon	fresh cilantro
1¹/2 teaspoons	salt

Put all the ingredients in a large nonreactive saucepan. Bring to a boil, stirring frequently. Reduce the heat and simmer for a further 20 minutes or so, occasionally stirring the mixture.

Remove the pan from the heat. Ladle the hot salsa into hot, sterilized, 1-pint jars, leaving ¹/4-inch headspace. Adjust the lids and process in a boiling-water bath for 15 minutes, following the method on page 20. Label and store the jars in a dark, cool place for at least a couple of weeks before using to let the flavors develop. Use within 12 months.

YELLOW TOMATO & SWEET CORN SALSA

FILLS 4 ½-PINT JARS

This is a lively and colorful alternative to the classic salsa. It is fabulous with a homemade hamburger, or a broiled skirt steak.

1	large mild onion, peeled and chopped
1 tablespoon	sunflower oil
1 pound	yellow tomatoes, halved, seeded, and chopped
1 or more	green or red chilies, seeded and finely chopped
½ cup	apple juice
1 cup	cider vinegar
1 cup	sugar
2 tablespoons	fresh coriander, chopped
2 tablespoons	fresh mint
1 teaspoon	salt
1 teaspoon	pepper
4 ears	fresh sweet corn

Gently fry the onion in the oil on low heat until soft, then add the tomatoes and chili. Raise the heat, then add the apple juice. Simmer the vegetables until just soft, then add the vinegar, sugar, herbs, seasoning. Cut the corn kernels from the ear with a sharp knife, then add. Continue cooking for a further 30 minutes until the mixture thickens, stirring occasionally.

Remove the pan from the heat. Skim any foam from the surface. Pour the salsa into hot, sterilized jars, and process them for 15 minutes in a boiling-water bath, following the method on page 20. Label and store the jars for at least a couple of weeks before using to allow the flavors to develop. Use within 12 months.

Vegetables

Here are two mixed vegetable recipes that are the staples of any store cupboard. One is a homemade version of Branston pickle, the strong-tasting British pickle that is made with green tomatoes. With its double dose of vinegar, this pickle keeps particularly well in hot climates. You can, of course, vary the vegetables according to what you have available, adding pumpkin, eggplant, and small squash if you prefer. You can also add chili or ginger for extra bite. The other is a sweet relish with cabbage and bell peppers, a favorite relish in Southern states. Serve it with beans and barbecue food.

GREEN TOMATO & MIXED VEGETABLE PICKLE

FILLS 7 1-PINT JARS

This is the classic filling for cheese and pickle sandwiches.

8	green tomatoes, diced
2	cucumbers, peeled, quartered lengthwise, and the watery core removed.
1	large onion, peeled and diced
1 pound	seedless raisins or sultanas
1 pound	French beans, trimmed and diced
8 to 10	celery stalks, washed and diced
8	carrots, peeled and diced
2 cups	salt
8 cups	distilled vinegar
1¼ cup	Demerara or a dark muscovado or molasses sugar
3 tablespoons	powdered mustard
3 tablespoons	flour
1 tablespoon	ground turmeric
2 teaspoons	ground allspice
4 cups	spiced vinegar—*see page 15*

Make a brine of 2 cups salt and 16 cups water. Place the vegetables in a large nonreactive bowl then cover with the brine for 24 hours. Drain well and cover with the unspiced vinegar for a further 24 hours. Drain the vegetables again, retaining the vinegar for future vegetable pickles if you wish.

Mix the sugar, mustard, flour, and spices to a paste with a little of the spiced vinegar in a nonreactive saucepan, then gradually stir in the remaining spiced vinegar until smooth. Add the prepared vegetables and simmer for 20 minutes.

Remove the pan from the heat. Skim any foam from the surface. Pot the pickle in hot, sterilized jars. Seal. Process in a boiling-water bath following the method on page 20. Label. Store in a cool, dry place. Use within 12 to 18 months.

SWEET CHOW-CHOW RELISH

FILLS 7 ½-PINT JARS

8 cups	shredded cabbage (about 1 medium head)
1	onion, finely chopped
1	green or red bell pepper
2 tablespoons	salt
2 cups	sweet vinegar—*see page 15*

Combine the vegetables in a nonreactive bowl and sprinkle with salt. Leave to stand for 4 to 6 hours in the refrigerator. Then take the bowl out of the chill and drain well.

Put the vegetables and the vinegar in a nonreactive saucepan and simmer for 10 minutes. Bring to a boil.

Remove the pan from the heat, then ladle the boiling hot vegetables into hot, sterilized jars. Seal. Process in a boiling-water bath, following the method on page 20. Label the jars and store in a cool dark place. Use within 12 to 18 months.

CHRISTMAS PRESERVES

An array of jars and bottles full of gleaming, jewel-like preserves has always been a feature of the holiday table. The early colonists brought with them festive traditions from all over Europe; many of these have survived to this Christmas season. Preserves such as mincemeat have stood the test of time, although the recipe has, naturally enough, changed over the decades. I have developed several easy, delicious mincemeat recipes that do not use beef suet, let alone minced beef (which was found in the earliest recipes). Instead, these new recipes of mine call for olive oil, canola oil, or creamed coconut. As well as being a major ingredient of traditional mince pies and tarts, hot mincemeat can be spooned over ice cream for an instant festive dessert. It is also a fabulous filling for baked apples and pears as a lovely rustic end to a holiday dinner party.

I have included both traditional and contemporary preserve recipes in this small chapter, from mincemeat to salsa, all of which are suitable for the holiday season. It is always worth making extra, some for your own Christmas table, and some to give as presents.

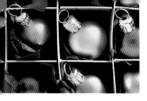
Apples

Instead of the usual mincemeat for Christmas, I have used some of the same ingredients to make a Christmas jam. The dried fruit is suspended in apple jelly instead of being bound with suet.

CHRISTMAS JAM

FILLS 6 1-PINT JARS

The jam is even more versatile than mincemeat, in that it is delicious on toast or warm scones. You can also use it in tarts and pies.

3 pounds	tart apples, such as Granny Smith, cut into wedges
6 cups	water
1 1/2 cups *each*	dried figs, dried apricots, dried pears, chopped
1 cup each	dried and pitted dates, chopped
1 cup each	dried and pitted prunes, chopped
1/4 cup	candied lemon peel
1/4 cup	candied orange peel
1/4 cup	candied cherries
	finely grated zest of 1 orange and 1 lemon
	juice of 1 orange and 1 lemon
1/2 teaspoon *each*	ground cardamom and cinnamon
1/2 teaspoon	anise
4 cups	sugar
1/2 cup	walnut pieces
1/2 cup	slivered almonds

Put the apples into a large nonreactive saucepan with the water and simmer until the fruit is soft. Put the chopped and pitted dried fruit in a large bowl. Press the apples with a potato masher, then spoon the mixture into a scalded jelly bag suspended over the large bowl, then leave to drip, without squeezing or forcing, overnight.

The next day, put the remaining ingredients, but not the nuts, into a large nonreactive saucepan and add the soaked, dried fruit. Stir, then simmer gently until the sugar dissolves. Bring to a boil, then boil for 5 minutes. Skim the surface, then add the nuts. Boil for a further 5 minutes or until the setting point is reached.

Remove the pan from the heat. Pot the jam in hot, sterilized jars. Process in a boiling-water bath following the method on page 20. Seal and label. Store in a cool, dry place. Use within 12 months.

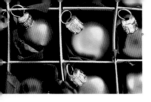

Cranberries

Each fall, starting mid-September and continuing through to Thanksgiving, growers harvest these delicious red berries. Unlike most fresh fruit, cranberries are at their peak during the holidays and will brighten any dish you serve.

CRANBERRY & CINNAMON JELLY

FILLS 6 ½-PINT JARS

Also try a spoonful of this clear, deep red jelly with broiled salmon or trout.

2 pounds	cranberries, fresh or frozen
2 cups	water
4	cinnamon sticks
2 cups	warm sugar to each 2 cups juice—*see recipe*

Put the cranberries in a nonreactive saucepan with the water and 3 cinnamon sticks, then simmer until the fruit is very soft, stirring occasionally until the sugar dissolves. Remove the cinnamon sticks, and squash the cranberries with a potato masher to extract as much juice and flavor as possible. Spoon the fruit and liquid into a scalded jelly bag or cheesecloth suspended over a large bowl, and let the juice strain through without forcing, for a few hours or overnight. Do not squeeze the bag or the jelly will be cloudy if particles of fruit escape into the liquid.

The next day, measure the juice into a nonreactive saucepan. Add the right amount of sugar and the remaining cinnamon stick. Stir the mixture over low heat until the sugar dissolves, then boil rapidly until the setting point is reached. Stir from time to time to prevent the sugar-rich mixture from sticking and burning.

Remove the pan from the heat. Skim any foam from the surface, then remove the cinnamon stick. Pot the jelly in hot, sterilized jars. Seal. Process the jars in a boiling-water bath, following the method on page 20. Label and store in a cool, dark place. Use within 12 months.

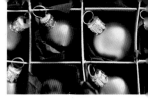

Figs

Dried figs are useful in preserves, such as chutneys, and I also like to use them in mincemeat. Traditional mincemeat is made in the fall for use at Christmas. It is best stored in the refrigerator, where it will keep for 3 to 4 months. Serve the mince pies to any brave carol singers who call!

FIG & APPLE MINCEMEAT

FILLS 4 1-PINT JARS

This delicious, rich-tasting mincemeat will keep well, since fresh apple is only added when you want to make mince pies; two medium, peeled, cored and grated tart apples, such as Granny Smith, are sufficient for about 2 pounds mincemeat.

1 pound	dried figs
1 pound	dried apples *(not apple crisps, but leathery rings of dried fruit)*
1 pound	mixed vine fruit, currants, raisins, and golden raisins
1 cup	candied peel, chopped
3/4 cup	chopped walnuts or almonds
1 cup	moist brown sugar
1/2 cup	apple cider brandy or calvados
1/2 cup	olive oil or coarsely grated, chilled, creamed coconut
1 teaspoon each	ground cinnamon and anise

Remove the stalks from the end of the figs, then chop them, and the dried apples, to roughly the same size as the vine fruits. Put the chopped dried fruit in a bowl, then stir in the remaining ingredients. Leave overnight for the flavors to blend. The next day, spoon the mixture into hot, sterilized jars, then seal and label the jars. Refrigerate and use within 4 months.

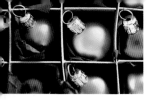

Dried Grapes

Dried grapes, collectively known as vine fruits, come in several varieties, depending on whether black or green grapes have been used, and which type of grape. Golden currants are dried green grapes, currants are dried black grapes, and raisins can be either grape. In California, for example, most raisins are produced from the Thompson seedless grape. Muscatel raisins are dried muscatel grapes, and are larger and more distinctively red than ordinary raisins.

Vine fruits are essential for mincemeat. Over the years, I have developed several recipes, many of which are suitable for, or adaptable for, vegetarians, as there are now many useful substitutes for beef suet, which was the traditional ingredient for enriching mincemeat when people stopped using minced meat. Vegetarian suet, olive oil, and coconut cream are just some of the alternatives you can use. My recipe is useful, because you make a basic recipe, and then add extra ingredients each time you want to use it.

A LA CARTE MINCEMEAT

FILLS 4 1-PINT JARS

Choosing extra ingredients from the list printed below the basic recipe means you can vary the intrinsic flavors of the mincemeat, which you can then use in individual mince pies, or in a larger tart, which would be the ideal accompaniment for a holiday buffet.

8 ounces	dried apricots or stoned prunes
8 ounces	raisins
8 ounces	dates
8 ounces	golden raisins
8 ounces	currants
3/4 cup	shredded beef or vegetarian suet
or 3/4 cup	canola oil
or 1 cup	grated coconut cream
1 cup	Demerara or moist brown sugar
1/2 cup	chopped mixed peel
	grated zest and juice of 1 lemon and 1 orange
1 teaspoon	ground mixed spice

1/2 teaspoon	ground cardamom
1/2 cup	rum or brandy
1/2 cup	sweet sherry or port

Chop or mince the dried fruit, then mix all the ingredients in a nonreactive bowl and leave, covered, for 24 hours before potting in hot, sterilized jars. Seal and label. Refrigerate for 3 to 4 months.

When you wish to use the mincemeat, spoon a generous cup into a bowl. That, together with one of the following, will fill 12 to 18 mince pies:

1 tart apple, such a Granny Smith, peeled, cored, and grated, then mixed with 1/2 cup slivered almonds

1 pear, peeled, cored, and grated, then mixed with 1 tablespoon freshly grated gingerroot, or stem gingerroot

1 tart apple, such as Granny Smith, peeled, cored, and grated, then mixed with a handful or two of dried cranberries, cherries, or blueberries

half a medium-sized pineapple, peeled, cored, and chopped, then mixed with a handful of pine nuts, finely chopped Brazil nuts, or desiccated coconut

1 fresh mango, peeled and chopped, then mixed with a handful of chopped cashew nuts

1 cup fresh or frozen cranberries in a little freshly squeezed orange juice cooked over low heat in a nonreactive saucepan, until they pop, then mixed with chopped mandarin segments and grated zest, or chopped kumquats

COOK'S NOTE: *If mixed ground spice is not available, you can make up your own version with equal quantities of ground cloves, cinnamon, nutmeg and ginger, adding ground allspice and ground mace if you can.*

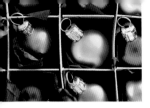

Citrus Fruit

By Christmas I have usually run out of Seville orange marmalade, so I then turn to seasonal clementines, tangerines, mandarins, and satsumas, combined with other citrus fruit, to make a well-flavored, well-set marmalade.

CHRISTMAS MARMALADE

FILLS 3 1-PINT JARS

12 clementines	skins only
3	lemons, juice and skins
2 cups	freshly squeezed pink grapefruit juice
3 cups	sugar, warmed

Cover the clementine skins with water in a nonreactive saucepan, then simmer on low heat until soft. Add the lemon skins, once you have squeezed and retained the juice. The membranes inside the lemons, and any pits, should be wrapped in a muslin parcel, together with any pits from the clementines, and simmered with the fruit skins.

When the skins are soft, finely chop, slice, or briefly process them, then put the mixture back in a nonreactive saucepan with the juice and cooking liquid. Reheat. When the mixture is hot, add the sugar, stirring until it dissolves, then bring to a boil and boil until the setting point is reached.

Remove the pan from the heat. Skim any foam from the surface. Pot the marmalade in sterilized hot jars. Process in a boiling-water bath following the method on page 20. Seal and label the jars. Store in a cool, dry place. Use within 12 months.

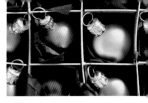

Dried Pineapple

Dried pineapple is available from healthfood stores and supermarkets, and it can be combined with fresh pineapple and other tropical fruits, both fresh and dried, in this luscious and luxurious mincemeat, which I feel sure our great-grandmothers would have loved, if they had had access to all the fabulous dried fruit available in most stores these days.

PINEAPPLE MINCEMEAT

FILLS 2 1-PINT JARS

SUITABLE FOR VEGETARIANS

Use this mixture for a tempting mincemeat tart, then serve it with rum-and-raisin ice cream as an alternative to Christmas pudding on the day.

1	lime, or lemon, rind scrubbed and grated
1 cup	moist brown sugar
3 cups	dried fruit, chopped small, chosen from the following: pineapple, mango, papaya, banana, or dates
1 1/2 cups	fresh fruit, finely chopped, chosen from the following: pineapple, physallis, guava, or mango
1/2 cup	creamed coconut, grated
3 tablespoons	chopped, blanched almonds
1/2 teaspoon *each*	ground cardamom, cinnamon, cloves, and mace
2 to 3 tablespoons	dark rum, optional

Squeeze the lime or lemon juice into a nonreactive bowl. Combine the rest of the ingredients well, then leave overnight, covered, for the flavors to blend. The next day, pot the mixture in hot, sterilized jars. Seal and label. Store in the refrigerator. Use within 12 months.

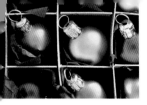

Tomatoes

Tomatoes are not at their best in the northern hemisphere at Christmas. I have discovered that combining them with other ingredients makes for a livelier New Year holiday salsa, as you can tell from the following recipe.

ROASTED RED SALSA

FILLS 2 ½-PINT JARS

This is an excellent relish to accompany cold cuts, such as ham or turkey. I always keep a bag of cranberries in the freezer so that I can use them throughout the year.

2	red tomatoes, quartered, roasted, skinned, and chopped
4	plum tomatoes, roasted, seeded, and chopped
4	red bell peppers, roasted, peeled, seeded, and diced
4 tablespoons	fresh or frozen cranberries, poached until soft
1 or 2	red chilies to taste, seeded and thinly sliced
1 teaspoon	cumin seeds
½ teaspoon	salt
½ cup	moist brown sugar
½ cup	wine vinegar
	finely chopped green or red chili, to taste

Put all the prepared ingredients into a nonreactive saucepan over low heat. Cook, stirring, until the sugar dissolves, then simmer for about 40 minutes until the mixture thickens.

Remove the pan from the heat. Skim any foam from the surface. Spoon the salsa into sterilized hot jars. Process in a boiling-water bath following the method on page 20. Seal and label the jars. Store in a cool, dry place. Use within 12 months.

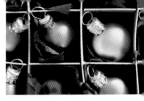

Rumtopf

A rumtopf is a variety of fruits mellowed in liquor and sugar in a stone crock for several months to "ripen." It is a simple and delicious method of preserving summer fruit. Rumtopf is the German word for "rum pot" which, of course, is what this recipe is—fruit preserved in rum. However, this century-old practice requires top quality fruit. It works best with organic fruit.

RUMTOPF

Build your selection throughout the fall, and you will have an excellent jar of fruit in liqueur to serve as an instant dessert during the festive season, and throughout the winter. Serve a spoonful of the fruit in a glass with a little of its liqueur. You can use apricots instead of cherries in this recipe.

2 pounds	cherries, rinsed and dried
4 cups	white rum, *eau-de-vie*, or vodka
2¹/₂ cups	sugar

Cut the cherry stems to ¹/₂ inch in length. Put the cherries, rum, *eau-de-vie,* or vodka in a large nonreactive bowl, stir in the sugar, then leave until the sugar dissolves, stirring occasionally. Put the cherries into a hot, sterilized jar, then cover with the liquid. Ideally, you should keep the fruit for a couple of months before broaching. As different fruits come into season, however, you can add a layer, and keep topping up with fruit, sugar, and spirit of choice throughout the summer. A tall, glass confectionery jar, such as those from old-fashioned candy stores, is ideal for creating a display of fruits in liqueur.

COOK'S NOTE: *As you add more fruit, remember to keep it covered in a mixture of spirit and sugar, in the proportions already given, which are 1 part sugar to 2 parts spirits, and 2 parts fruit.*

INDEX

The BookMaker would like to thank everybody involved with this book, especially Frances Bissell for agreeing to write it, to Amanda Hancocks for her photographs that make everything seem delicious, and to Mary for her luscious design. Thanks are also due to Stuart Busby of Chef's Connection, New Covent Garden, for the best fruit and vegetables.

For more information on preserves and canning, visit the United States Department of Agriculture website, www.usda.gov.